Yielding My Best For His Glory

Bishop R S Walker

Yielding My Best For His Glory

Copyright © 2013 by Bishop R. S. Walker

Published by:

Bishop R. S. Walker Ministries
2760 Crain Highway
Waldorf, MD 20601
Voice: (301) 843-9267 FAX: (240) 585-7093
http://www.bishoprswalker.com
Email: admin@bishoprswalker.com

ISBN-13: 978-0692435106
ISBN-10: 0692435107

Printed in the United States of America

Dedication

This journal is dedicated to my lovely wife, Pastor Betty A. Walker. She has been an extraordinary blessing to me and provides tremendous support with all of my writing projects. Her encouragement and assistance, in every area of preparation, is greatly appreciated. Thank you Betty! I could not do this without you.

Acknowledgements

Thank You...To my son, Rodrick Walker, for your contribution in developing the cover of the journal. To Elder Carla Aultmon, for your contributions with cover development of this publication. To Elder Cynthia V. White for your support and assistance in preparing the journal for publication. I appreciate your willingness to meet the challenges necessary to prepare this product for printing and distribution. To Elder Moira Washington for your help in the edit and format of this publication. To Deacon Lisa Burgess for your help and support in proofing this publication. To my son, Rodney S. Walker, Jr., for your constant support and contribution on this project. To Elder Vicki Browning for your continued assistance in the office during the times I am writing and your interception of problems that may arise. Thank God for your tremendous gift of problem solving. To my daughter-in-law, Natasha Walker, for all the care and support she gives to my son, Rodrick, as he works overtime, in many cases from home, to complete these projects.

Introduction

This Devotional **"Yielding My Best for His Glory"** is designed to assist you in developing an intimate life with the Lord. It will position you where you can hear God clearer and have a real sense of following His lead into a time of worship and into a life consecrated to Him and for Him. In order for me to do that personally, **I had to position myself where I was "Yielding My Best for His Glory.**

I will lead you through a twenty-one week consecration and fasting before the Lord as **directed by God.** In order to build the kind of discipline that is necessary for hearing God clearly and obediently, consecration is a must. What does that mean? Those that commit to doing this consecration are agreeing to commit to shutting off the television, radio and anything else that could contaminate your hearing and will do so for twenty-one consecutive weeks, engaging in nothing that does not involve the Lord. It is clear and I do understand that you have to work and interact with people. This is all part of developing the discipline needed for an intimate relationship with the Lord. During this consecration and mentoring sessions, you will develop a different heart, a heart that does not make you replace God with man or anything else. This means you are developing a closer relationship with God that is consistent with the Word of God.

The First Four-Week Period focuses on examples in books, chapters and verses of the Bible where God spoke to people that He was pleased with. Emphasis will mainly be placed on the four gospels. It is very important that you see:

1. God's nature in how He spoke.
2. Principles that governed how God moved.
3. What moved God
4. Laws that govern the earth
5. Ways God communicated with His people (through an audible voice, impressions, visions, dreams, etc...)

The Second Four-Week Period focuses on how you hear and what prevents you from hearing accurately. It is important for you to see your heart and its condition. Creating a clean heart is very important as God cannot get through an unconditioned heart. In this time you will ask God to create in you a clean heart and renew a right spirit in you. The word says, "from out of the abundance of the heart the mouth speaks." Therefore, you have to see what's in your heart so you are not confused in your understanding and thereby speaking the wrong things.

The Third Four-Week Period focuses on your ability to listen, how to listen and practice listening. Because you will be fasting some kind of fast during this consecration, discipline will not really be a challenge. You will start the process of living a fasted life beginning the first week. Now in this third four week period, you will find out how important it is to listen deeply and communicate what you hear. This is the time you will learn to say what the Lord is saying and not what it seems as if the Lord is saying.

The Forth Four-Week period focuses on listening to God to see what He is saying to you and about you. Oftentimes, you think that God is trying to say something to you regarding other people, but on the contrary God really desires to talk to you about you. God will begin to minister to you about areas in your life that need correction. It may be things you know about and things you have no knowledge of. You should have an accountability partner and you will have to ask them if they can see those things in your life. Throughout this period, God will talk to you about things He desires you to do, like giving money for good causes, buying someone lunch and the list goes on. This is to get you to the place where you have no price. This is when you start to give up things you may not have regularly given up. Remember everything God will have you to do will never violate anyone, their space, life, property or anything that belongs to someone else. God is a God of order, a God of design and a God of objectivity.

The Fifth and Final Period will consist of five weeks and the major focus will be on hearing what God is saying and sharing what you heard. This period will be a period of fine tuning and judging the word you've received from the Lord. When a word is judged, it positions you for a place of being favored by and increasing in the knowledge of the Lord.

Get ready to **yield your best for His glory** and be transformed into the image of God's Son through the renewing of your mind and living a consecrated and fasted life.

God is Calling; Are You Listening?

As He was walking by the Sea of Galilee, He noticed two brothers, Simon who is called Peter and Andrew his brother, throwing a dragnet into the sea, for they were fishermen. And He said to them, Come after Me [as disciples— letting Me be your Guide], follow Me, and I will make you fishers of men! At once they left their nets and became His disciples [sided with His party and followed Him]. Matthew 4:18-20 AMP

Week 1　　　　**Day 1** _____

_____

As Jesus began His earthly _____

Ministry, he needed some to _____

assist him and called Simon _____

Peter and Andrew, His brother. _____

He asked them to follow Him. _____

Those words are really more _____

powerful than we may realize. _____

What this really means is to _____

follow him in whatever He was

going to do, whatever He was **Prayer Focus:** *Are you listening? What is God*

going to go through and where *saying? What is He asking of you?*

ever He was going. There are _____

times we are challenged with this _____

level of the call. It is not a call into _____

ministry but a call to follow Him. _____

As you go through this day _____

examine how close you are _____

following Jesus' example in _____

action and deed. _____

_____

_____

_____

_____

_____

_____

_____

1

God is Calling; Are You Listening?

As He was walking by the Sea of Galilee, He noticed two brothers, Simon who is called Peter and Andrew his brother, throwing a dragnet into the sea, for they were fishermen. And He said to them, Come after Me [as disciples— letting Me be your Guide], follow Me, and I will make you fishers of men! At once they left their nets and became His disciples [sided with His party and followed Him]. Matthew 4:18-20 AMP

Week 1   **Day 2**

_____
_____
_____
_____
_____
_____
_____
_____
_____
_____
_____
_____

Prayer Focus: Gauge youself on how clear you have heard today. Commit Matthew 4:18-20 to memory.

There was a yielding that His disciples had to embrace, and that means swiftly yielding to the desires of their Lord. If we say He is Lord (Master, Ruler and Controller of our life), then we should swiftly follow him, not causally. The word "follow" means to be in the same way with, that is, to accompany (specifically as a disciple). Examine your life closely! Are you in the same way with Him?

_____
_____
_____
_____
_____
_____
_____
_____
_____
_____
_____
_____
_____
_____

God is Calling; Are You Listening?

As He was walking by the Sea of Galilee, He noticed two brothers, Simon who is called Peter and Andrew his brother, throwing a dragnet into the sea, for they were fishermen. And He said to them, Come after Me [as disciples— letting Me be your Guide], follow Me, and I will make you fishers of men! At once they left their nets and became His disciples [sided with His party and followed Him]. Matthew 4:18-20 AMP

Week 1   **Day 3**

When Jesus called James and John they obeyed at once. There is something about instant obedience verses obeying in time. Often we find ourselves waiting to obey God. There is a hunger in the heart of God and an eagerness in God waiting to see us instantly obeying Him. Do you find your will still getting in the way when it is time to immediately obey God? Anything that is less than instant obedience is disobedience. God eagerly awaits your obedience to His will. What part of your will have you broken today?

_____
_____
_____
_____
_____
_____
_____
_____
_____
_____
_____

Prayer Focus: Is what you are hearing today in your prayer time, supported by the word of God or the will of God?

_____
_____
_____
_____
_____
_____
_____
_____
_____
_____
_____
_____
_____

3

God is Calling; Are You Listening?

If you are willing and obedient, you shall eat the good of the land; Isaiah 1:19 REMIND PEOPLE to be submissive to ir] magistrates and authorities, to be obedient, to be prepared and willing to do any upright and honorable work, Titus 3:1 AMP

Week 1   **Day 4**

_____

_____

_____

_____

_____

_____

_____

_____

_____

_____

_____

_____

Prayer Focus: *Think about the ways that God has spoken to you. Write about it!*

_____

_____

_____

_____

_____

_____

_____

_____

_____

_____

_____

_____

_____

_____

_____

_____

*God says, **"If you are willing and obedient, you shall eat..."** When you and I are willing to do what is required, it is like a drink offering being poured out on the behalf of someone else. Your will is required of you. As we embrace the call of God to ascend into discipleship, there are things that we must share regarding Jesus. We must share in the dying of Christ, the resurrection of Christ and the joy of Christ. The dying of the Lord is the breaking of your will.*

Remember, "submission" is not a dirty word as the "Dove" is not a dirty bird.

4

God is Calling; Are You Listening?

Let this mind be in you, which was also in Christ Jesus: Who, being in the form of God, thought it not robbery to be equal with God: But made himself of no reputation, and took upon him the form of a servant, and was made in the likeness of men: and being found in fashion as a man, he humbled himself, and became obedient unto death, even the death of the cross.   *Philippians 2:5-8 KJV*

Week 1   **Day 5** _____

_____

Here is how you break your will and shift into this new place in God. You "let this mind be in you which was also in Christ Jesus." The word "Let" is a word of permission, which causes you to allow something to happen that would not have permission otherwise. God said in the beginning, "Let there be light!" and there was (Genesis 1:3). Nothing can become, if you don't let it. You can break your will, if you let it break. This will be a good time to fast a day and ask God to break that difficult thing in your life that seems not to go away.

Prayer Focus: What was the hardest part in this week for you to get past? That will be the same place that the enemy will try to fortify in your will, while you are trying to break it. How will you prevent him? Make the agreement and have your accountability

_____

_____

_____

_____

_____

_____

_____

_____

_____

_____

_____

_____

_____

What Will You Die To?

Then Jesus came from Galilee to the Jordan to John to be baptized by him. But John protested strenuously, having in mind to prevent Him, saying, "It is I who have need to be baptized by You, and do You come to me?" But Jesus replied to him, "Permit it just now; for this is the fitting way for [both of] us to fulfill all righteousness [that is, to perform completely whatever is right]." Then he permitted Him. Matthew 3:13-15 AMP

Week 2   **Day 1**

_____
_____
_____
_____
_____
_____
_____
_____
_____
_____
_____

When God speaks or desires to do so, many times your lack of submission to the one you are called to submit under causes you not to hear God as clear as well as you could. In Matthew Jesus encountered His first test: the test of submission. John recognizes the greatness of Jesus and knew Jesus had something He could do for him, but Jesus realized the purpose of God. Therefore, He knew He had to submit to John if He was to have a right to ministry, have God to speak of Him, and overcome temptation in the wilderness.

Prayer Focus: Ask the Father if there is anyone you know that you should be submitting to. If there is, there is a great challenge deep down on the inside of you because you are not dead enough to your will. There is a dying in you that must take place or the voice of God will remain mute

_____
_____
_____
_____
_____
_____
_____
_____
_____
_____
_____
_____
_____
_____

6

What Will You Die To?

Then Jesus came from Galilee to the Jordan to John to be baptized by him. But John protested strenuously, having in mind to prevent Him, saying, "It is I who have need to be baptized by You, and do You come to me?" But Jesus replied to him, "Permit it just now; for this is the fitting way for [both of] us to fulfill all righteousness [that is, to perform completely whatever is right]." Then he permitted Him. Matthew 3:13-15 AMP

Week 2   **Day 2**

*Jesus says something so powerful while submitting to John; **"Suffer it to be so now."** The Amplified says, **"Permit it just now."** These words are words of life and destiny. Jesus is saying to John, can you just permit this for this moment knowing that God will say something in the next hour that permits (allows, sets in motion) something that you have no control over. **"Permit it just now;"** says this is a dying moment. Jesus submitted to John even though John was not as gifted, anointed or as smart. This was the moment when John was in authority and Jesus gave way to John's moment by saying, **"Permit it just now."** The real question is who has God called you to submit to at this moment? Who will you **"permit it just now?"***

Prayer Focus: *Whose moment do you have to give way to? How does it make you feel knowing you could do things so much better than they can, but you are to give way? This is a dying moment for you. Can you gracefully kill your flesh and permit their moment to be?*

7

What Will You Die To?

And going on further from there He noticed two other brothers, James son of Zebedee and his brother John, in the boat with their father Zebedee, mending their nets and putting them right; and He called them. At once they left the boat and their father and joined Jesus as disciples [sided with His party and followed Him].   Matthew 4:21-22

Week 2   **Day 3**

_____
_____
_____
_____
_____
_____
_____
_____
_____
_____
_____

Prayer Focus: If you listen closely, you'll hear God telling you how to die to your will and to live to His. What decision do you have to now make to die to your will?

_____
_____
_____
_____
_____
_____
_____
_____
_____
_____
_____
_____
_____
_____

Jesus said, *"Perform whatever is right."* Then He submitted and permitted him to do what was right. Sometimes there is a battle that goes on in you to rebel against something, even though you know what is right. What is that? That is called being only human; yet God is calling you higher than the human level of operation. You can decide to stay at a human level or you can *"perform completely what is right"*. You can perform it or you can completely perform it. To do that which is right, there is a dying that must take place. Dying to your will is to be alive to the will of God. Dying to your will is to live the will of another. *"Always carrying about in the body the dying of the Lord Jesus, that the life of Jesus also may be manifested in our body. For we who live are always delivered to death for Jesus' sake, that the life of Jesus also may be manifested in our mortal flesh."* 2 Corinthians 4:10-11 NKJV

What Will You Die To?

But we have this treasure in earthen vessels that the excellence of the power may be of God and not of us. We are hard-pressed on every side, yet not crushed; we are perplexed, but not in despair; persecuted, but not forsaken; struck down, but not destroyed— always carrying about in the body the dying of the Lord Jesus, that the life of Jesus also may be manifested in our body. For we who live are always delivered to death for Jesus' sake, that the life of Jesus also may be manifested in our mortal flesh. So then death is working in us, but life in you. 2 Corinthians 4:7-12 NKJV

Week 2   **Day 4**

What did Jesus realize that we often do not? Jesus realized the same thing that Paul spoke about. Paul talked about the treasure we have in earthen vessels. We will discover in this 21 weeks what that treasure is and that is activated by the power of submission, which creates the dying of the Lord. Paul said, **"We who are alive are always delivered unto the death of Jesus."** Why? God helping us to die to our will is the only way we can live to the power of God.

Prayer Focus: Can you identify the ways and the things God wants you to die to? There are things that bother you and there are things that don't faze you at all. Whatever controls your emotions are the things God desires to kill in your life.

What Will You Die To?

But we have this treasure in earthen vessels that the excellence of the power may be of God and not of us. We are hard-pressed on every side, yet not crushed; we are perplexed, but not in despair; persecuted, but not forsaken; struck down, but not destroyed— always carrying about in the body the dying of the Lord Jesus, that the life of Jesus also may be manifested in our body. For we who live are always delivered to death for Jesus' sake, that the life of Jesus also may be manifested in our mortal flesh. So then death is working in us, but life in you. 2 Corinthians 4:7-12 NKJV

Week 2　　　　　**Day 5**

_____

_____

_____

_____

_____

_____

_____

_____

_____

_____

_____

_____

You must change how you look at the things that happen to you. Paul said, "We are hard pressed on every side, yet not crushed." Being hard pressed does not mean we have sinned nor does it mean we are not of God. Everyone experiences being hard pressed. The challenge is how we see what is happening. You are always hearing about the dying of Lord. Something within you needs to die yet at the same time you need to see what is happening as an opportunity to advance. "How you see the problem is the problem" not because the problem came. 2 Corinthians 4:10-11 NKJV

Prayer Focus: Make this the day you change how you will look at things that happen to you. Dale Carnegie stated, "If life delivers you a lemon, make lemonade." Don't allow the day to turn sour. Remember God can speak through any situation if you only listen while you are in it.

_____

_____

_____

_____

_____

_____

_____

_____

_____

_____

_____

_____

_____

But, What is God Saying?

THEN JESUS was led (guided) by the [Holy] Spirit into the wilderness (desert) to be tempted (tested and tried) by the devil. And He went without food for forty days and forty nights, and later He was hungry. And the tempter came and said to Him, "If You are God's Son, command these stones to be made [loaves of] bread." Matthew 4:1-3 AMP

Week 3   **Day 1**

_____
_____
_____
_____
_____
_____
_____
_____
_____
_____
_____
_____

By this time after so much fasting, no doubt that you have been tested on every hand and some level of discouragement may have set in without you realizing what happens when you fast. But don't buy into the discouragement. This is the time that your fasting is really beginning to work. When you fast, challenges come to prove or test you. Use the tests to identify your level of growth or accepted discipline. When you fast you are also chipping away at the things that have once controlled you. On the other side, you are becoming more sensitive to God. Therefore, you can't let discouragement win. This is when you fight the good fight of faith and lay hold of salvation. Jesus fought the good fight of faith and stood on the Word. Did you notice that Satan never came until Jesus was hungry or vulnerable? Satan will try you the same way.

Prayer Focus: What stand will you take when Satan shows up to try you at your most vulnerable point? Will you fight the good fight of faith or will you cave in and quit? Quitters never win and winners never quit. Quitting is not an option!

_____
_____
_____
_____
_____
_____
_____
_____
_____
_____
_____
_____
_____
_____

But, What is God Saying?

THEN JESUS was led (guided) by the [Holy] Spirit into the wilderness (desert) to be tempted (tested and tried) by the devil. And He went without food for forty days and forty nights, and later He was hungry. And the tempter came and said to Him, "If You are God's Son, command these stones to be made [loaves of] bread." Matthew 4:1-3 AMP

Week 3   **Day 2**

Prayer Focus: In what way will you be "alert?" In what way will you be watchful?

When you are fasting for certain results, don't fall prey to Satan's absence. Don't let up because you don't feel any pressure. Satan is not always present. Today's scripture says, **"and Satan came."** The KJV says, **"and when the tempter came, he said."** This is an indication that the tempter is not always present. The things that you have always been vulnerable to more than likely will always be the thing that Satan will return with. **1 Peter 5:8 NKJV** says, **"Be sober, be vigilant; because your adversary the devil walks about like a roaring lion, seeking whom he may devour. Resist him, steadfast in the faith, knowing that the same sufferings are experienced by your brotherhood in the world."** The word "vigilant" means to be watchful and "Sober" means to be alert. Therefore, be watchful and alert so you don't fall prey to the tricks of the Devil.

12

But, What is God Saying?

THEN JESUS was led (guided) by the [Holy] Spirit into the wilderness (desert) to be tempted (tested and tried) by the devil. And He went without food for forty days and forty nights, and later He was hungry. And the tempter came and said to Him, "If You are God's Son, command these stones to be made [loaves of] bread." Matthew 4:1-3 AMP

Week 3   **Day 3**

Do you know you are a child of the living God? Do you know you are made in the image of God? When Satan comes, one of the first things he tries to do is to get you to doubt who you by questioning your identity. If he can ever get you to question your identity, he has a major part of the battle won. Jesus never doubted who He was, even though Adam did. In **Matthew 3** God said, **"This is my beloved Son in whom I am well pleased."** If Jesus had not submitted to John, he still would have been the Son of God. However, he would have been the Son of God without power; no standing power. During this phase of the consecration, guard your identity.

Prayer Focus: Take the stand! Know who you are and whose you are! Don't doubt it for one moment! Say with me; "I am a child of God! I am seated in Heavenly places in Christ Jesus. I am more than a conqueror through Christ Jesus. I am a believer! I am not a doubter." See how many "I am" scriptures you can find.

13

But, What is God Saying?

But He replied, "It has been written, Man shall not live and be upheld and sustained by bread alone, but by every word that comes forth from the mouth of God." Matthew 4:4 AMP

_____

_____

_____

_____

_____

_____

_____

_____

_____

_____

Prayer Focus: Stay on the cutting edge with the word. God will do a new thing and He will speak about the new thing. Write the word God is now speaking in your spirit

_____

_____

_____

_____

_____

_____

_____

_____

_____

_____

_____

_____

_____

_____

_____

_____

Week 3   **Day 4**

Jesus replied in a way we should never forget, **"Man shall not live and be upheld and sustained by bread alone, but by every word that comes forth from the mouth of God."** Matthew 4:4 AMP. The KJV says, **"but by every word that proceedeth out of the mouth of God."** There is a preceding word, but God warns us to live by every word that proceeds out of the mouth of God. The preceding word is the one already spoken, but the proceeding word is the one He is yet to speak, the word that gives new definition and new direction to His will.

14

But, What is God Saying?

But He replied, "It has been written, Man shall not live and be upheld and sustained by bread alone, but by every word that comes forth from the mouth of God." Matthew 4:4 AMP

Week 3   **Day 5** _____

The reality is you are upheld by the Word of His power. If you let the Word uphold you, you will find yourself walking at a level that the enemy can't touch you. To what degree do you stand on the word when God speaks to you? When you stand on the Word, healing comes in your body and deliverance comes to your mind. Every day you should be standing on a Word from God. Sometimes the Word might be something God spoke to you out of the Bible or it may be an impression in your spirit. However God gives it to you, stand on it. The word is quick and powerful and sharper than any two-edged sword. Never doubt the Word because it has creative ability.

Prayer Focus: Use this day to create something by the power of your words. You will be amazed how things happen. Yes, God will even use you to do something miraculous. Write about it.

15

Embrace Your Gethsemane

Then cometh Jesus with them unto a place called Gethsemane, and saith unto the disciples, "Sit ye here, while I go and pray yonder." And He took with Him Peter and the two sons of Zebedee, and began to be sorrowful and very heavy. Then saith He unto them, "My soul is exceeding sorrowful, even unto death: tarry ye here, and watch with me." Matthew 26:36-38 KJV

Week 4   **Day 1**

Do you ever sense that God desires more from you and that He is calling you into a deeper place? What do you do at those times? Sometimes God requires more from you even in times when you do not think there is any more to give. But because God knows you, He pushes you to the extent of teaching you how to tap into your overflow. It is like an olive, for example. You think the olive is at its best when it is eaten as food. God, however, shows you that its real value is at the point of its crushing. It is at that time that a valuable oil seeps from it. The most valuable part of your existence is realized at the point of your crushing.

Prayer Focus: *Have you been pushed enough where your valuables have been seen? Push past the pressure until you see the new you; the one not even you have met.*

16

Embrace Your Gethsemane

Then cometh Jesus with them unto a place called Gethsemane, and saith unto the disciples, "Sit ye here, while I go and pray yonder." And He took with Him Peter and the two sons of Zebedee, and began to be sorrowful and very heavy. Then saith He unto them, "My soul is exceeding sorrowful, even unto death: tarry ye here, and watch with me." Matthew 26:36-38 KJV

Week 4   **Day 2**

Have you ever gone to a place and knew that it was the place where your spiritual death would happen? This place is one of your greatest conflicts just before the major one. When you come to that place, you will know it because it is a place of challenge and the place that pulls you into purpose. This is the moment that you welcome your dying day. God has a desire to extract the oil from you so that your value can be seen. However, before that can happen, you have to say yes! Say yes to the will of God no matter how painful it may be. It is your dying place where you die like never before so you can live like never before. This is the place where you say, "Nevertheless, thy will be done!

Prayer Focus: Let your mind, spirit and soul say, yes! Jesus said, "Nevertheless." Peter said, "Nevertheless." Now it is your turn to say, "Nevertheless." Identify your current challenges and practice saying "nevertheless" and "yes" to the will of God."

17

Embrace Your Gethsemane

Then cometh Jesus with them unto a place called Gethsemane, and saith unto the disciples, "Sit ye here, while I go and pray yonder." And He took with Him Peter and the two sons of Zebedee, and began to be sorrowful and very heavy. Then saith He unto them, "My soul is exceeding sorrowful, even unto death: tarry ye here, and watch with me." Matthew 26:36-38 KJV

Week 4   **Day 3**

_____

_____

_____

_____

_____

_____

_____

_____

_____

_____

_____

Prayer Focus: *This is your moment to part from things that have meant the most to you. What things or people will you give up for Him (Your Lord and Savior)?*

_____

_____

_____

_____

_____

_____

_____

_____

_____

_____

_____

_____

_____

_____

The word "nevertheless" could be one of the most painful words you will ever say. This is when God asks you to give up something you really desire to keep. There comes a parting in the soul from the thing you have become so attached to. It could even be a relationship; but whatever it is, you have to die to it. Now you come to Gethsemane and God is requiring this relationship of you so that you can see Him at a level you have never experienced before. Your Gethsemane may represent the place that only three people in your life can go with you and even they don't successfully handle it. You find yourself all alone with them and it feels like you are without them.

Embrace Your Gethsemane

Then cometh Jesus with them unto a place called Gethsemane, and saith unto the disciples, "Sit ye here, while I go and pray yonder." And He took with Him Peter and the two sons of Zebedee, and began to be sorrowful and very heavy. Then saith He unto them, "My soul is exceeding sorrowful, even unto death: tarry ye here, and watch with me." Matthew 26:36-38

Week 4　　　　**Day 4**

"My Soul is exceedingly sorrowful even unto death. Watch with me." Jesus had one request of the three that are the closest to Him. He wanted them to help pray Him through this one. Have you ever just needed someone to be there with you just to make it through the storm and they failed? There is a place in God you have to go alone. When you meet with dying moments, you may have to go alone. Is your soul exceedingly sorrowful because of the expectation of this kind of death? When you let things go that are dear to you but hazardous to your destiny, it hurts down in your soul.

Prayer Focus: Are you willing to endure the present suffering for future glory? Do it gracefully!

19

Embrace Your Gethsemane

Then cometh Jesus with them unto a place called Gethsemane, and saith unto the disciples, "Sit ye here, while I go and pray yonder." And He took with Him Peter and the two sons of Zebedee, and began to be sorrowful and very heavy. Then saith He unto them, "My soul is exceeding sorrowful, even unto death: tarry ye here, and watch with me." Matthew 26:36-38

Week 4   **Day 5**

Sometimes we die unnecessary deaths because we do not consider the people that we have or don't have around us that are our confidants. A confidant is "a person with whom one shares a secret or private matter, trusting them not to repeat it to others." Jesus had three confidants Peter, James and John. In this dying place, you have to have accountable individuals whom you can confide in to reveal where you are in that moment whether it is spiritually, mentally, emotionally or whatever the hard place you are dealing with. This place is designed to make you better.

Prayer Focus: Lord show me my confidants as I go through my dying place in my life. I yield my best for your glory! If "my best" means my dying to me, let your will be done in my life.

Let The Glory Be Revealed

For I reckon that the sufferings of this present time are not worthy to be compared with the glory which shall be revealed in us. For the earnest expectation of the creature waiteth for the manifestation of the sons of God.
Romans 8:18-19 KJV

Week 5   Day 1

How well do you see into the coming glory that is destined for you? Sometimes you are deeply challenged by the sufferings you meet at certain periods of growth. Many times you run from the sufferings you go through because you start to measure the suffering with what you think others did not have to go through. God is pushing you not to measure the suffering with others, but to measure the suffering you are going through with the glory you are about to obtain at the appointed time God has set on His calendar. Godly sufferings equal the glory of God. When God's glory shows up, it hides you from the enemy that at one point tried to kill you. Your desire should be to be clothed with the glory of God that once clothed Adam and the woman.

Prayer Focus: Push past the suffering to the glory of God. Father in this season, I will no longer measure my success in you by other people and what they seem to have accomplished in life. I will measure my success by what I am willing to endure that brings your glory in my life. Help me to never complain about where I am, but to keep pressing into the next place you are calling me into.

21

Let The Glory Be Revealed

For I reckon that the sufferings of this present time are not worthy to be compared with the glory which shall be revealed in us. For the earnest expectation of the creature waiteth for the manifestation of the sons of God.
Romans 8:18-19 KJV

Week 5   **Day 2**

_____

_____

_____

_____

_____

_____

_____

_____

_____

_____

Every day **"yield your best"** to access the glory of God. You now realize that the whole creation is waiting on you to manifest as a son of God. Complaining about where you are and what you are going through does not bring the glory of God. The Word of God says, **"Though He were a son, yet learned He obedience by the things He suffered."** In this season you must yield your vessel to God and not keep yielding to your vessel. Let this be the week that you yield and give up all the things your vessel is craving and calling for, such as cake, sweets and not exercising. What shall you give?

Prayer Focus: I yield my best for His glory! I give my best for His best! My undisciplined soul shall not bring me captive again to the things that once controlled me. Yes, I give myself away to Jesus so He can use me!

_____

_____

_____

_____

_____

_____

_____

_____

_____

_____

_____

_____

_____

_____

_____

Let The Glory Be Revealed

For the creature was made subject to vanity, not willingly, but by reason of him who hath subjected the same in hope, Because the creature itself also shall be delivered from the bondage of corruption into the glorious liberty of the children of God. For we know that the whole creation groaneth and travaileth in pain together until now. Romans 8:19-21

Week 5   Day 3

There are ways you are subjected to vanity, but not willingly. Many times you may find yourself challenged in areas that seem to control you. These are areas you have to conquer. Identify the things that seemingly have you locked down and always in bondage. There is a breaking out that must happen in order for you to reach a place of liberty in God. There is sometimes a struggling that takes place in the flesh that must be done until you are free. There is a God-kind of fast that must be realized to bring you into this liberty. The more you tap into God and His power, the more liberated you will become. Fasting brings truth into your reality and truth brings freedom in a manifested form.

Prayer Focus: I realize that "the man I feed the most will be the one that wins at the end!" Therefore I commit myself to a fasted life. A fasted life is a life where you are always in some kind of fasted situation. I will fast meats, sweets, coffee, TV, Facebook, Twitter, the computer and anything else that has proven it has me addicted. Decree in this season, "Nothing shall have dominion over me for I am **"yielding my best for His glory!"**

Let The Glory Be Revealed

For the creature was made subject to vanity, not willingly, but by reason of him who hath subjected the same in hope, Because the creature itself also shall be delivered from the bondage of corruption into the glorious liberty of the children of God. For we know that the whole creation groaneth and travaileth in pain together until now. Romans 8:19-21

Week 5   **Day 4**

You will be delivered into the glorious liberty of the children of God and now you are looking for the manifestation of it. Something must break the outer shell of what has held you captive. Your ability to fast, pray and use the faith God has given you to penetrate the next dimension will break the shell. There is a place in God that Satan would love to keep you out of. Remember, **"The kingdom of heaven suffers violence and the violent take it by force."** There is only one way to penetrate this next place and that is to violently take it in the realm of the spirit.

Prayer Focus: Put on your warfare cry and violently assault the thing that holds you captive. If it is pride, greed, lust, or whoredom, violently attack it!

24

Let The Glory Be Revealed

For the creature was made subject to vanity, not willingly, but by reason of him who hath subjected the same in hope, Because the creature itself also shall be delivered from the bondage of corruption into the glorious liberty of the children of God. For we know that the whole creation groaneth and travaileth in pain together until now. Romans 8:19-21

Week 5   **Day 5** _____

_____

"For we know that the whole creation groaneth and travaileth in pain until now." If you are ever going to come out of your bondage, you have to groan, travail and cause a shift in the spirit realm until change comes. This is where your prayer language will come in. If you don't know how to speak in tongues, now is a good time to find out how. But until then, there is what I call a belly cry. This is where you intensify all your prayer efforts. Did you know you can give birth to an amazing move of God in the earth?

Prayer Focus: There was a cry that the children of Israel did in Egypt that caused heaven to move. Your cry causes heaven to move. There is a shift that takes place in the earth where it concerns you. This cry is by faith and it moves earth! In Acts 16:26, Paul and Silas prayed at midnight and caused the move on earth. Cry out to God by faith until there is a shift and a change in your life.

_____
_____
_____
_____
_____
_____
_____
_____
_____
_____

25

Identify Your REAL Enemies

Do you not know that those who run in a race all run, but one receives the prize? Run in such a way that you may obtain it. And everyone who competes for the prize is temperate in all things. Now they do it to obtain a perishable crown, but we for an imperishable crown. Therefore I run thus: not with uncertainty. Thus I fight: not as one who beats the air. But I discipline my body and bring it into subjection, lest, when I have preached to others, I myself should become disqualified. 1Corinhian 9:24-27

Week 6   **Day 1**

_____
_____
_____
_____
_____
_____
_____
_____
_____
_____
_____

Prayer Focus: *During this season aggressively confront and attack your real enemy! This year will be your freest year. Declare this as your year of freedom for freedom belongs to you.*

_____
_____
_____
_____
_____
_____
_____
_____
_____
_____
_____
_____
_____

Don't fight as one that beats the air, or as one with no purpose. Every fight you have should be one that counts. Satan is good at influencing you to think you are fighting things you are not fighting. He will have you fighting symptoms and not root causes. You may find yourself staying away from water, men, women, airplanes, relationships, marriage, etc. Satan will cause you to miss out on life's pleasures by camouflaging the real enemy, fear. Yes, Satan uses fear as his tactic and had you believing the enemy was marriage, relationship, water, airplanes and etc. He had you shut down from life and life never was an enemy.

Identify Your REAL Enemies

Do you not know that those who run in a race all run, but one receives the prize? Run in such a way that you may obtain it. And everyone who competes for the prize is temperate in all things. Now they do it to obtain a perishable crown, but we for an imperishable crown. Therefore I run thus: not with uncertainty. Thus I fight: not as one who beats the air. But I discipline my body and bring it into subjection, lest, when I have preached to others, I myself should become disqualified. 1Corinhian 9:26-27

Week 6   Day 2

There have been times in my life where I knew I was losing a battle that the enemy had called me to. I was fighting against an enemy that I had let in and gave access to me. Shutting that enemy down in my life was the difficult part because no one was preaching or teaching about it. Then I heard the Apostle Paul say in 2 Corinthians 10:4, "For the weapons of our warfare are not carnal but mighty in God for pulling down strongholds, casting down arguments and every high thing that exalts itself against the knowledge of God, bringing every thought into captivity to the obedience of Christ,". At that point, I knew I could win my battle if I took responsibility for what was happening to me.

Prayer Focus: Who do you need to stop blaming for the battle you are losing right now? Start aiming at the real enemy in your life. You can find that real enemy by looking at the door you left opened and identifying what came in.

Identify Your REAL Enemies

Do you not know that those who run in a race all run, but one receives the prize? Run in such a way that you may obtain it. And everyone who competes for the prize is temperate in all things. Now they do it to obtain a perishable crown, but we for an imperishable crown. Therefore I run thus: not with uncertainty. Thus I fight: not as one who beats the air. But I discipline my body and bring it into subjection, lest, when I have preached to others, I myself should become disqualified. 1Corinhian 9:26-27 NKJV

Week 6   **Day 3**

_____

_____

_____

_____

_____

_____

_____

_____

_____

_____

You are competing for the prize of your freedom. How many things exist in your life that you are deliberately not disciplining? What is out of control in your life that you know you can bring under control, but you are not doing anything about it? "And everyone who competes for the prize is temperate in all things." Since there are things that drive you, start using discipline with the things you know you are ignoring. You are competing for the prize, therefore become temperate in all things. Discipline your flesh in the obvious areas.

Prayer Focus: *Start deeply listening to God. Many times God speaks softly in your spirit telling you what not to do so you would win. Pause for six-seconds between every decision you make because that one decision may lock you down for ever. What is it that you have neglected to deal with that is keeping you from obtaining your freedom?*

_____

_____

_____

_____

_____

_____

_____

_____

_____

_____

_____

28

Identify Your REAL Enemies

Do you not know that those who run in a race all run, but one receives the prize? Run in such a way that you may obtain it. And everyone who competes for the prize is temperate in all things. Now they do it to obtain a perishable crown, but we for an imperishable crown. Therefore I run thus: not with uncertainty. Thus I fight: not as one who beats the air. But I discipline my body and bring it into subjection, lest, when I have preached to others, I myself should become disqualified. 1Corinthian 9:26-27

Week 6   Day 4

Do you find yourself being inconsistent in the things of God, when you have a desire to be consistent? I often see people who I know want to obey God, but they keep running into the same walls over and over. One of the greatest reasons they are so challenged is because they have no one to expose their enemy to. Pride keeps you from exposing your enemy. Your enemy is not a person. The Bible says, **"For we do not wrestle against flesh and blood, but against principalities, against powers, against the rulers of the darkness of this age, against spiritual hosts of wickedness in the heavenly places."** Ephesians 6:12. NKJV. Your enemy is anger. Attack the anger; not the person.

Prayer Focus: If there is not something living in you that connects you to the enemy you hate, then there would be no battle. Find the connector that lives in you and crush it under your feet. Fasting reveals the connectors and shuts them down so that they no longer operate.

Identify Your REAL Enemies

Do you not know that those who run in a race all run, but one receives the prize? Run in such a way that you may obtain it. And everyone who competes for the prize is temperate in all things. Now they do it to obtain a perishable crown, but we for an imperishable crown. Therefore I run thus: not with uncertainty. Thus I fight: not as one who beats the air. But I discipline my body and bring it into subjection, lest, when I have preached to others, I myself should become disqualified. 1Corinhian 9:26-27 NKJV

Week 6   **Day 5**

_____

_____

_____

_____

_____

_____

_____

_____

_____

_____

_____

Prayer Focus: During this season aggressively confront and attack your real enemy! This year will be your freest year. Declare this as your year of freedom for freedom belongs to you.

_____

_____

_____

_____

_____

_____

_____

_____

_____

_____

_____

_____

_____

Don't fight as one that beats the air, or as one with no purpose. Every fight you have should be one that counts. Satan is good at influencing you to think you are fighting things you are not fighting. He will have you fighting symptoms and not root causes. You may find yourself staying away from water, men, women, airplanes, relationships, marriage, etc. Satan will cause you to miss out on life's pleasures by camouflaging the real enemy, fear. Yes, Satan uses fear as his tactic and had you believing the enemy was marriage, relationship, water, airplanes and etc. He had you shut down from life and life never was an enemy.

F.O.C.U.S.

Create in me a clean heart, O God, And renew a steadfast spirit within me. Do not cast me away from Your presence, And do not take Your Holy Spirit from me. Restore to me the joy of Your salvation, And uphold me by Your generous Spirit. Psalm 51:10-12 NKJV

Week 7   Day 1

How clean is your heart? How pure are your thoughts? Do you wrestle with fleshly thoughts on a regular basis? Most people never think about how they think and that is one is of Satan's biggest strategies against the people of God. Yet, everyone at some point have dealt with the nagging thoughts. David asked the Lord to create in him a clean heart and renew the right mind in him. There were thoughts David had challenges with, but he said something that gave me understanding. David spoke about his being shaped in **iniquity** and born in **sin**. These are key words that brings understanding on today's challenges. There are also sins that live in your genes that have been passed down from your parents. But, it is good to know that even those sins can be overcome.

Prayer Focus: There are steps you have to make today in order to get your life back. You swing directly at the driving force. Be specific in your fighting. Today you must aim right at your enemy and not against anyone else you would like to blame. What driving forces do you need to confront?

31

F.O.C.U.S.

Create in me a clean heart, O God, And renew a steadfast spirit within me. Do not cast me away from Your presence, And do not take Your Holy Spirit from me. Restore to me the joy of Your salvation, And uphold me by Your generous Spirit. Psalm 51:10-12 NKJV

Week 7   **Day 2**

_____
_____
_____
_____
_____
_____
_____
_____
_____
_____

David asked God to create in him a steadfast spirit. Is your spirit steadfast or are you somewhat wishy washy? The word steadfast means to be unmovable, always abounding; not swift to change positions. There was something in the heart of David that caused him to shift according to what he felt. You have to watch out for things that take away your focus. You have to create a sense of focusing and overcoming unusual setbacks. (F.O.C.U.S.) There are things that would set you back, but the power of F.O.C.U.S will put you over every time. What are some of the setbacks that you have to conquer or bounce back from?

Prayer Focus: *Start today creating a steadfast heart by meditating on the Word day and night. It is at that time you will begin to make your way prosperous and you will start having good success. Do it Now and Win.*

_____
_____
_____
_____
_____
_____
_____
_____
_____
_____
_____

F.O.C.U.S.

Create in me a clean heart, O God, And renew a steadfast spirit within me. Do not cast me away from Your presence, And do not take Your Holy Spirit from me. Restore to me the joy of Your salvation, And uphold me by Your generous Spirit. Psalm 51:10-12 NKJV

Week 7   Day 3

"Do not take Your Holy Spirit from me. Restore to me the joy of Your salvation, And uphold me by Your generous Spirit." Every time you sin something dies and joy is lost. Because David sinned, he ask God not to take the Holy Spirit away from him. He knew that the Holy Spirit brings the joy, salvation and steadfastness, which creates the F.O.C.U.S. Keep the Holy Spirit on assignment in your life and the F.O.C.U.S. will be there. You have to continue **"yielding your best for His glory,"** otherwise you never begin to experience the salvation, deliverance and the freedom of the Lord. Let God reaffirm His power in your life through the presence of His Holy Spirit. Nurture your relationship with the Holy Spirit through meditating on the Word and increase your level of F.O.C.U.S.

Prayer Focus: Get back your steadfast heart and will to win. Secondly, recreate your level of focus.

33

F.O.C.U.S.

Create in me a clean heart, O God, And renew a steadfast spirit within me. Do not cast me away from Your presence, And do not take Your Holy Spirit from me. Restore to me the joy of Your salvation, And uphold me by Your generous Spirit. Psalm 51:10-12 NKJV

Week 7　　　　**Day 4**

_____

_____

_____

_____

_____

_____

_____

_____

_____

_____

_____

Prayer Focus: Will you give God your life today? I am not talking about accepting Him as Lord and Savior. Jesus says to the Church in Revelation 3:20, "Behold I stand at the door and knock, if any man will open to me I will come in..." Will you yield and let Jesus in?

_____

_____

_____

_____

_____

_____

_____

_____

_____

_____

_____

_____

_____

David said to God, **"Uphold me by Your generous Spirit."** There is something that happens when you yield yourself to God. One of the greatest tragedies within the body of Christ is that we don't yield ourselves to God as Christ did. When you are challenged with yielding, you miss seeing the generous hand of the Spirit of God. For that reason, you hear preaching that says, "he may come when you want him;," which is not in the Bible anywhere. When you latch onto unbiblical clichés, you are not yielding. The reason they say things like that is because they are unyielding not because He is unwilling

F.O.C.U.S.

Behold, I stand at the door, and knock: if any man hear my voice, and open the door, I will come in to him, and will sup with him, and he with me. Revelation 3:20

Week 7   Day 5

By this time your level of intimacy has increased and you are moving towards sensitivity in your relationship with Him. Yielding should come just a little easier by now. By now you should know that it does not take a crisis to come into a yielded place in God. "With loving kindness have I drawn thee," is what he says. He loves you so much that you are literally drawn to Him by his love. Since God has drawn you, what will you give Him? Will you give yourself as a yielded vessel? There is a sweet smell that you bring to the nostrils of God when you yield to Him. One of the reasons God stepped to the Apostle Paul on the road to Damascus was to give him the opportunity to yield. God is giving you the same opportunity.

Prayer Focus: Are you interested in causing Jesus to come in and "sup" with you? Jesus desperately desires to come in and fellowship with you but, do you make him feel welcome? Yielding is like an invitation to Jesus. Let Jesus come in.

35

Identify Your Battleground

"And from the days of John the Baptist until now the kingdom of heaven suffereth violence, and the violent take it by force". Matthew 11:12

_____

_____

_____

_____

_____

_____

_____

_____

_____

_____

_____

Prayer Focus: Identify what your struggles, challenges, and difficulties are and where they have been coming from. There are things in this season you do have to fight, but where is the battle ragging is the question. Begin to seek God about the direction of your battle. Whatever ground you have to take, take it by force.

_____

_____

_____

_____

_____

_____

_____

_____

_____

_____

_____

_____

_____

Week 8   Day 1

It is important for you to understand that the enemy does not desire you to enter this level of freedom. Therefore, the enemy knows he lost some ground with you. Now you have to be sure you always keep this level of freedom no matter what! Most of us are not aware of our battle ground or where the attack or challenge is coming from. We have not been taught to do battle or stand against challenges. No wonder we are clueless of where it's coming from. We have been trained to receive blessing and all good things, which is good. However, we have to know there is an enemy out there and at one point or another, you will need to fight or stand against him. Please be advised you will not always have to fight as in warfare, but sometimes it may be the good fight of faith. Another time it may be a serious battle, where you have to take something by force; **"And from the days of John the Baptist until now the kingdom of heaven suffereth violence, and the violent take it by force".** Matthew 11:12 During this time be watchful that you don't lose the ground you have gained.

36

Identify Your Battleground

"And from the days of John the Baptist until now the kingdom of heaven suffereth violence, and the violent take it by force". Matthew 11:12

Week 8 **Day 2**

_____
_____
_____
_____
_____
_____
_____
_____
_____
_____
_____
_____
_____

You are in a battle right now and you have already fought some battles. Some you have won, some you lost and some you feel like you did not win or lose; you were just engaged in a fight. Why would you lose any battle when God says you are more than a conqueror? Two major reasons for defeat is that you 1) did not understand the battle ground or 2) have been lured on fighting grounds that you were not called to, and consequently ended up looking like a defeated foe. You are not defeated foes; you simply did not understand what you were fighting for or why you are even engaged in the battle. Any battle that you go into and you neglect to understand, it must be repeated.

Prayer Focus: What enemy is fighting you at this level? You are not where you use to be; you have grown even though it doesn't seem like it. This where you decide what you are no longer going to do. Let this be a time where you challenge yourself on doors you opened that gave the enemy.

_____
_____
_____
_____
_____
_____
_____
_____
_____
_____
_____
_____
_____
_____
_____

Identify Your Battleground

"And from the days of John the Baptist until now the kingdom of heaven suffereth violence, and the violent take it by force". Matthew 11:12

_____
_____
_____
_____
_____
_____
_____
_____
_____
_____
_____

Prayer Focus: *Watch the things that you have an appetite for. It could be anything, food, sex, wealth, marriage, etc. Those are the things Satan uses as drawing tools to lure you into battles of your defeat.*

_____
_____
_____
_____
_____
_____
_____
_____
_____
_____
_____
_____
_____
_____
_____

Week 8   **Day 3**

Have you been seduced by your enemy? Seduction is something that draws you in, entices you or tempts by deceit; usually by things that you are attracted to. You were seduced by an enemy that suckered you into a battle. The only thing that you have ever heard was that the mind (internal) was the battleground. You have been taught for years that your mind was the battleground and that is all you understood. Please understand that it is only one of the battle-grounds. But before the enemy can get that close, you have to be seduced into coming close enough where he can have access to your mind. There are things the enemy has used that are enticing to you. Those are the things that keep you bound. You are from the kingdom of light and Satan desires to draw you into his kingdom of darkness. Remember, "every man is tempted when he is drawn away and enticed." James 1:15 When you are drawn away (not lead), you are seduced. Check out the meaning of the word seduce.

38

Identify Your Battleground

For though we walk in the flesh, we do not war after the flesh: 4(For the weapons of our warfare are not carnal, but mighty through God to the pulling down of strong holds;) 5 Casting down imaginations, and every high thing that exalteth itself against the knowledge of God, and bringing into captivity every thought to the obedience of Christ; 2 Corinthians. 10:3-5

Week 8   Day 4

Stay in a place of intimacy and meditation with the Lord. Intimacy has a way of changing your mind or will. God wants the mind of Christ to operate in you. The will of Christ is synonymous or kin to the mind of Christ. Operating In the mind of Christ is contingent upon you surrendering to His thoughts. God would love to have you thinking through His mind and doing exactly what He says. During this period of consecration, God will give you the opportunity to think through His mind and to operate in His power. When God initially gave me that opportunity, I knew I had to *"Yield My Best For His Glory"*. I had to give my best to function in the realm of His power and splendor (glory). Will you do likewise?

Prayer Focus: Let your focus be to discipline yourself so that you have power against any agent that will try to lure you where you should not go or to participate in that which you should not. What measure of discipline will you use today? What kind of fast are you doing to this week? This is one of your methods of discipline.

Identify Your Battleground

For though we walk in the flesh, we do not war after the flesh: 4 (For the weapons of our warfare are not carnal, but mighty through God to the pulling down of strong holds;) 5 Casting down imaginations, and every high thing that exalteth itself against the knowledge of God, and bringing into captivity every thought to the obedience of Christ; 2 Corinthians. 10:3-5

Week 8   **Day 5**

_____
_____
_____
_____
_____
_____
_____
_____
_____
_____

Prayer Focus: To be delivered from you people or things you must:
1.   *Keep God First*
2.   *Do That Which Pleases God*
3.   *Yield Your Best for His Glory*

_____
_____
_____
_____
_____
_____
_____
_____
_____
_____
_____

We live in a very different reality and the only real stars are the ones that God makes, not the one we make ourselves. Desiring to glorify God keeps you from being lured into places you do not belong. The late Apostle Betty Peebles coined the phrase, "Performing for an Audience of One." Think about that. How many people are you performing for? How many are you trying to prove something to? If you look at the life of Jesus, you will see that He lived what she put into words. Jesus was performing for an audience of one - His Father God. Jesus would always say, **"I came to do the will of my Father or I say only what I hear Him say."** He was performing for an audience of one Jesus says in **John 6:38 "For I came down from heaven, not to do mine own will, but the will of him that sent me."** He was performing for an audience of one. Get delivered from people! Don't allow anyone or anything to have that much power over you where you perform for them or it. If you understand this, you will have victory. God will lead you into the state of blessing during this 21 weeks of consecration.

Developing Intimacy With God

This book of the law shall not depart out of thy mouth; but thou shalt meditate therein day and night, that thou mayest observe to do according to all that is written therein: for then thou shalt make thy way prosperous, and then thou shalt have good success. Joshua 1:8 KJV

Week 9   Day 1

God has a great desire to communicate with His people. Yet one of our greatest challenges is to stay in a place of intimacy and meditation with the Lord. The word says, **"Meditate upon the word day and night then you will make your way prosperous and then you will have good success."** If there is no meditation on the word day and night, then there will be no success in what you are after. God has a desire to bring you into His fullness, but it can only happen through meditation of the word. One reason God wants you to meditate on the word is because that coupled with worship brings about intimacy. Intimacy is the place God can more clearly speak to you. Jesus, after nearly every time of ministry went in to a solitary place to pray and refresh in that place of intimacy again. Intimacy with God is what brings success in ministry, business and in your personal lives.

Prayer Focus: Create a time of intimacy with God as you consecrate and give yourself to Him this week. Come against all distraction, time thieves and hindrances that will show up to steal the time you set aside for God,

41

Developing Intimacy With God

Create in me a clean heart, O God, And renew a steadfast spirit within me. Do not cast me away from Your presence, And do not take Your Holy Spirit from me. Restore to me the joy of Your salvation, And uphold me by Your generous Spirit. Psalm 51:10-12 NKJV

Week 9　　　　　**Day 2**

_____

_____

_____

_____

_____

_____

_____

_____

_____

_____

_____

Prayer Focus: The Truth exposes lies any time you desire to see truth. Commit yourself today to hear truth and eliminate every lie of the enemy.

_____

_____

_____

_____

_____

_____

_____

_____

_____

_____

_____

_____

_____

Stay in a place of intimacy and meditation with the Lord. Intimacy has a way of changing your mind or will. God wants the mind of Christ to operate in you. The will of Christ is synonymous or akin to the mind of Christ. Operating In the mind of Christ is contingent upon you surrendering to His thoughts. God would love to have you thinking through His mind and doing exactly what He says. During this period of consecration, God will give you the opportunity to think through His mind and to operate in His power. When God initially gave me that opportunity, I knew I had to *"Yield My Best For His Glory"*. I had to give my best to function in the realm of His power and splendor (glory). Will you do likewise?

Developing Intimacy With God

This book of the law shall not depart out of thy mouth; but thou shalt meditate therein day and night, that thou mayest observe to do according to all that is written therein: for then thou shalt make thy way prosperous, and then thou shalt have good success. Joshua 1:8 KJV

Week 9   **Day 3**

Let this place of intimacy and meditation with the Lord transform your thoughts and assist you in conforming into the image of God's dear son. Most of the time you become like your environment and that being the case, why not change the atmosphere around you? Create a place that is conducive for God to speak. If your atmosphere changes, your words will change; and if your words change, then your image will also. If the image you see changes, your world will change. God has a desire to bring you into the very image of His son, the Word. If God is going to be able to bring you into His image, your thoughts have to become His thoughts and His words have to become your words. As the word says, **"my thoughts are not your thoughts and my ways are not your ways."**

Prayer Focus: Your thoughts will determine your direction; therefore, how you submit your mind or will to Christ determines the degree to which you will walk in the image of Jesus?

43

Developing Intimacy With God

In whom the god of this world hath blinded the minds of them which believe not, lest the light of the glorious gospel of Christ, who is the image of God, should shine unto them. 2 Corinthians 4:4

Week 9   **Day 4**

_____

_____

_____

_____

_____

_____

_____

_____

_____

_____

_____

_____

Today is a moment of self-examination. Let's look at how well and to what degree you are being conformed into the image. To what degree are your thoughts changing? One favorite author of mine said, "the problems you have cannot be solves with the same mind that created them." Therefore, we enter a different level of intimacy and meditation with God so that our word would change. Your words are going to determine the next thing is to what degree are you changing in how you respond to situations. The image or your imagination is an indicator of your thought process. Is your thought process still the same? Can you deal with the situations you are confronted with and not be overtaken by your emotions?

Prayer Focus: All stinking thinking must change. Check out the way you are thinking and make sure you are not thinking out of your emotions. Remember, when you think out your emotions, your thoughts are not properly balanced. This is your time to advance, but your emotions will hold advancement back.

_____

_____

_____

_____

_____

_____

_____

_____

_____

_____

_____

_____

_____

_____

44

Developing Intimacy With God

Behold, I stand at the door, and knock: if any man hear my voice, and open the door, I will come in to him, and will sup with him, and he with me. Revelation 3:20

Week 9　　　　Day 5

How are your thoughts in this season? Do your thoughts match what God is saying regarding your life? There is an enemy that has always competed with what God has desired to do. Unfortunately, you are in that mix. Therefore, the enemy has desired to throw you down because he can't get to God. Because God has protected you, the enemy has gone the route of trying to deceive you into letting him into your thoughts processes. Satan tries to plant thoughts in your mind to gain access. Satan sends deceptive thoughts to your mind to blind your mind from the truth of God. So when the good or truth of the Word comes and you have given Satan access, you are blinded from the revealing of the truth. Remember Apostle Paul said, **"let this mind be in you."** If you have to let it be in you, then you could let a lie be there as well.

Prayer Focus: The Truth exposes lies any time you desire to see truth. Commit yourself today to hear truth and eliminate every lie of the enemy.

Fine Tuning Your Hearing

Then said I, Woe is me! for I am undone; because I am a man of unclean lips, and I dwell in the midst of a people of unclean lips: for mine eyes have seen the King, the Lord of hosts. Then flew one of the seraphims unto me, having a live coal in his hand, which he had taken with the tongs from off the altar: And he laid it upon my mouth, and said, Lo, this hath touched thy lips; and thine iniquity is taken away, and thy sin purged. Also I heard the voice of the Lord, saying, Whom shall I send, and who will go for us? Then said I, Here am I; send me. Isaiah 6:5-8

Week 10　　　　　**Day 1**

_____

_____

_____

_____

_____

_____

_____

_____

_____

_____

_____

Prayer Focus: This may be hard a thing, but necessary for the health of your relationship with God. Look out among your relationships, are there any toxic relationships you have to get rid of? Do you have things in your life you have to shut down? God is speaking, but are you listening.

Have you ever been in a situation where you have desired to hear God, but there were so many other things in the way blocking your ability to hear? **"In the year that king Uzziah died I saw also the Lord sitting upon a throne, high and lifted up, and his train filled the temple."** Many of us in these days have the same issue of hearing and seeing what God is doing. Isaiah said, in the year that King Uzziah died, **"I saw the Lord."** What is it that is in your life that represents King Uzziah, which blocks you from hearing or see what God is saying? This is a time you have to deal with things that hinder your process and blocks your ability. Can you see past the toxic relationship you are in? It may just be people that are going contrary to where God is taking you. Isaiah knew that he had to make some decisions about who was in in his life that was hindering his ability to see God for himself.

_____

_____

_____

_____

_____

_____

_____

_____

_____

_____

46

Fine Tuning Your Hearing

In the year that king Uzziah died I saw also the Lord sitting upon a throne, high and lifted up, and his train filled the temple. Above it stood the seraphims: each one had six wings; with twain he covered his face, and with twain he covered his feet, and with twain he did fly. Isaiah 6:1-2

Week 10   Day 2

Have you ever really thought about how difficult it is to deeply listen? There are times you have so many distractions in the way that prevents you from properly hearing. Sometimes you can't hear God over their voices of the people in your ear. Your hearing affects how you see. God confronts Isaiah on what he sees. If you are seeing right, then more than likely your hearing is right. Jesus asked a question, **"Who do men say that I the son of man am?"** After they responded Jesus ask, **"But whom do you say I am?"** Jesus wanted to know if their listening was affected by their hearing. I wonder if your listening has been affected by your hearing. What is the difference? Some people deeply or intently listen, while others just hear the words you used.

Prayer Focus: *Listen clearly to what God wants revealed through His Word before you try to hear what He is saying to your inner man. Whatever God speaks to your inner man must be judged by the word you carry with your outer man.*

Fine Tuning Your Hearing

Then said I, Woe is me! for I am undone; because I am a man of unclean lips, and I dwell in the midst of a people of unclean lips: for mine eyes have seen the King, the Lord of hosts. Then flew one of the seraphims unto me, having a live coal in his hand, which he had taken with the tongs from off the altar: And he laid it upon my mouth, and said, Lo, this hath touched thy lips; and thine iniquity is taken away, and thy sin purged. Also I heard the voice of the Lord, saying, Whom shall I send, and who will go for us? Then said I, Here am I; send me. Isaiah 6:5-8

Week 10　　　　**Day 3**

_____

_____

_____

_____

_____

_____

_____

_____

_____

_____

_____

_____

Prayer Focus: Will you give yourself to God in exchange for His friendship towards you? God shares details with those He can call loyal friends. At what level will you give yourself to the Lord? At the Judas level? How about at the Thomas level? If that is the extent of your commitment, then no wonder God will not speak to you as one speaks to a friend.

After having such an encounter with God, Isaiah realized what every one of us realize, that he was undone. Not only does he realize his own condition, but he also realized the condition of those that he was giving most of his time to. Isaiah says he was undone and that he dwelt among people that are undone. That was the reason for his unusable condition. Are you unusable because of those you give your time to? Are there bad ways bringing something on you that would not normally be there? When you come into the presence of a Holy God, your condition becomes evident. Understanding your condition pushes you to give yourself to God at a different level.

_____

_____

_____

_____

_____

_____

_____

_____

Fine Tuning Your Hearing

In the year that king Uzziah died I saw also the Lord sitting upon a throne, high and lifted up, and his train filled the temple. Above it stood the seraphims: each one had six wings; with twain he covered his face, and with twain he covered his feet, and with twain he did fly. Isaiah 6:1-2

Week 10   Day 4

When you are committed to God, you become willing to do what is necessary for the relationship to advance. Isaiah realized his condition and shifted from that condition to positioning himself in the process for development. What a price for clearer hearing - a live coal, and hot I might add! There are times you need something to burn off something that is stuck on. When I used to work on cars, I remember times when I tried to remove a part that had been on for a long time. The only way to get it unstuck, was to burn it off. Isaiah had unclean lips stuck to him and God's recipe was a live hot coal placed on his lips. Whoever God will us, must first be purified. If God is going to speak to you, then He expects that you will be willing to be used.

Prayer Focus: Honor of the Word brings on power from the Word. Whatever word God will have you to speak, He wants it honored. But who will honor a word that comes from a vessel that has not been purified? Spend some time today correcting the impure thoughts you think that makes your words impure. The impure thoughts come from an impure heart. And nothing can purify the heart like a fiery trial

Fine Tuning Your Hearing

Then said I, Woe is me! for I am undone; because I am a man of unclean lips, and I dwell in the midst of a people of unclean lips: for mine eyes have seen the King, the Lord of hosts. Then flew one of the seraphims unto me, having a live coal in his hand, which he had taken with the tongs from off the altar: And he laid it upon my mouth, and said, Lo, this hath touched thy lips; and thine iniquity is taken away, and thy sin purged. Also I heard the voice of the Lord, saying, Whom shall I send, and who will go for us? Then said I, Here am I; send me. Isaiah 6:5-8

Week 10   **Day 5**

Two things were necessary for Isaiah's hearing to become perfected. First, iniquity must be taken away. Iniquity are sins passed down through your bloodline through the genes. What kind of things or unbelief has been passed down your blood line? How long will they hinder your process in God? This is the time where you have to get rid of anything that hinders. Secondly, sin must to be purged. Sin will hinder your hearing every time. God said, **"this has touch thy lips and thine iniquity is taken away and thy sin is purged."** Hearing starts at the point of realizing that you are in right standing in your relationship with the Lord. Hearing increases when you set your heart to obey God at that level of hearing.

Prayer Focus:
1. *Come face to face with where you are*
2. *Accept the process God has chosen*
3. *Walk with a sin-free conscience*

Embrace The Peace Of God

Verily, verily, I say unto you, He that entereth not by the door into the sheep-fold, but climbeth up some other way, the same is a thief and a robber. But he that entereth in by the door is the shepherd of the sheep. To him the porter openeth; and the sheep hear his voice: and he calleth his own sheep by name, and leadeth them out. And when he putteth forth his own sheep, he goeth before them, and the sheep follow him: for they know his voice. And a stranger will they not follow, but will flee from him: for they know not the voice of strangers. John 10:10

Week 11   Day 1

If you will ever hear God clearly, you will have to remove all outside interferences and move your head and heart to a place of silence. As it is said in golf "quiet your hands and heart." Don't permit your inner world to be noisy. Jesus said, **"I leave with you my peace; I give unto you not as the world giveth."** Jesus also says, **"Let not your hearts be troubled neither let it be afraid"** God can speak under any circumstances. The question is; can you hear under any circumstances? Quiet your heart until you learn how to hear when there are many sounds that are trying to distort what God is saying in your world. Remember: Satan's job is be sure you never hear. If he is successful, you will always stumble in the dark. However if your ever embrace peace that God gives, you will walk in the light as Jesus is the light and will no longer stumble in darkness nor stumble at the darkness you see.

Prayer Focus: What is the circumstance that takes peace from you and prevents you from hearing? Where is God in all the noise you hear in the rattling of your soul? How do you quiet your soul and launch into peaceful habitation? The answer to these questions lie with you and what you are willing to do.

Embrace The Peace Of God

Peace I leave with you, my peace I give unto you: not as the world giveth, give I unto you. Let not your heart be troubled, neither let it be afraid. John 14:27
Verily, verily, I say unto you, He that entereth not by the door into the sheep-fold, but climbeth up some other way, the same is a thief and a robber. But he that entereth in by the door is the shepherd of the sheep. To him the porter openeth; and the sheep hear his voice: and he calleth his own sheep by name, and leadeth them out. And when he putteth forth his own sheep, he goeth before them, and the sheep follow him: for they know his voice. And a stranger will they not follow, but will flee from him: for they know not the voice of strangers. John 10:10

Week 11   **Day 2**

_____

_____
_____
_____
_____
_____
_____
_____
_____
_____
_____
_____

Prayer Focus: Your thoughts will determine your direction. Therefore, how submitted are you to the mind of Christ? What things do you think on that will bring the peace of God in your life? As you go through your process today and come across things in your life, let peace rule.

Think of all the things that has come to trouble your heart. All the time you were in control of your heart, you did not take control. Jesus said **"Let not your heart be troubled."** The word "Let" is a word of permission that says you have the power to permit things to be or to move things from being. As you attempt to hear God in a way that you have never heard before, let this be the time you must learn the power of the word "Let." What are the rules of the word "Let?"

- Laugh in your heart
- Exit all interferences
- Trim all your rough edges

_____
_____
_____
_____
_____
_____
_____
_____
_____

Embrace The Peace Of God

Verily, verily, I say unto you, He that entereth not by the door into the sheepfold, but climbeth up some other way, the same is a thief and a robber. But he that entereth in by the door is the shepherd of the sheep. To him the porter openeth; and the sheep hear his voice: and he calleth his own sheep by name, and leadeth them out. And when he putteth forth his own sheep, he goeth before them, and the sheep follow him: for they know his voice. And a stranger will they not follow, but will flee from him: for they know not the voice of strangers. John 10:10

Week 11   Day 3

Could one of the challenges to hearing be that there has not been any establishment of relationship between you and the good Shepherd? God has portrayed Himself in this story as the shepherd, and us as the sheep. He speaks of us being sheep that know the voice of the shepherd. Sheep and shepherds spend much time together; therefore, they know each other. Sheep spend time quietly listening to the voice of the shepherd. Yet, quiet is one of the things that most of us run from in this time. Think of the blessed quietness you experience when there is no television, no radio, and no social networks causing your thought to go up another notch - just the peace of Jesus where you are pushed into a place hear his voice. God does not yell as he speaks to us just a whisper that He may never repeat. Are you listening to the direction He is giving?

Prayer Focus: Father create in us a heart that is quiet enough to hear what you are not yelling. Speak to us from the peace you give. Teach us to hear and teach us to listen that we may how to follow your lead. We know you are saying something. We just cannot tell what it is.

Embrace The Peace Of God

The Lord is my shepherd; I shall not want. He maketh me to lie down in green pastures: he leadeth me beside the still waters. He restoreth my soul: he leadeth me in the paths of righteousness for his name's sake. Psalms 23:1-3

_____ **Week 11   Day 4**

_____

_____

_____

_____

_____

_____

_____

_____

_____

_____

_____

Prayer Focus: God eliminate everything out of this person's life that is following this 21 week plan of change. Whatever takes peace from them, Father I pray you would move it. Teach them to enter your rest by the still waters of life. Now Holy Father, I speak the peace of God to their spirit man and let your breath breathe on their situation.

The "Lord is our shepherd." Those words within itself are designed to lead you into a peaceful place; a place where the enemy is not able to defeat you because of the words God released to you. As long as you walk in those words, you have peace. But if you walk in the words of another, there will not be any peace. John said, **"a stranger they will not follow."** Are the words you are following those of peace? Do they describe the still waters? If you will hear his voice, you will have to get where the water is still. How about the waters of your mind? Do you rest in the fact that Jesus is your Shepherd? The sheep obey the voice of the Shepherd and that increases the level of peace you experience.

_____

_____

_____

_____

_____

_____

_____

_____

_____

_____

_____

_____

_____

_____

Embrace The Peace Of God

The Lord is my shepherd; I shall not want. He maketh me to lie down in green pastures: He leadeth me beside the still waters. He restoreth my soul: he leadeth me in the paths of righteousness for his name's sake. Psalms 23:1-3

Week 11   **Day 5** _____

There is a place of rest and it is called by the still waters. David said, **"He maketh me to lie down in green pastures: He leadeth me beside the still waters. He restoreth my soul: he leadeth me in the paths of righteousness for his name's sake."** Still waters, lying down and restore my soul are all things that will spell peace even in the life of those that are coming from a life of "the shadow of death." God desires to change that. But we have to hear God and then follow what God says. Why? Because He leads us into peace to re- store our soul. Now I am not sure if you heard that clear enough. All of the above are prerequisites for creating a place or atmosphere where you can hear God. Still waters that refresh, Paths of righteousness and lying down is an indication of you trusting your shepherd.

Prayer Focus: Master meditating on the Word and being quiet before Him. God teach us how to lay down before you and listen to your heart beat - yielding every one of our member as instruments of service to you.

55

What Price Are You Willing To Pay?

And the LORD spake unto Moses, saying, Speak unto Aaron and unto his sons, saying, On this wise ye shall bless the children of Israel, saying unto them, The LORD bless thee, and keep thee: The LORD make his face shine upon thee, and be gracious unto thee: The LORD lift up his countenance upon thee, and give thee peace. And they shall put my name upon the children of Israel; and I will bless them. Numbers 6:23-27

Week 12   **Day 1**

You have come to a place where God would put another demand on you. This time as you attempt to go higher in the presence of God, there has come a door of opportunity. Every time God ask you for something or ask you to do something, He also prepares something for you to receive. God asked Moses to bring His people out of Egypt and into the promise land. Then God prepared a grace for Moses to walk in. God told Jeremiah to speak to His people and I will be with your mouth. God is asking you to do something as well, but as He did with Abraham, He does not tell you all you will go through, what the total cost will be or what the blessing will be. God is asking you to give yourself to him at another level.

Prayer Focus: *What are you willing to do at this next level in Him? What are prepared to do for God and at what level will you submit? To hear God, you have to be willing to pay whatever it cost!*

What Price Are You Willing To Pay?

*And for Aaron's sons thou shalt make coats, and thou shalt make for them girdles, and bonnets shalt thou make for them, for glory and for beauty. **And thou shalt put them upon Aaron thy brother, and his sons with him; and shalt anoint them, and consecrate them, and sanctify them, that they may minister unto me in the priest's office.** And thou shalt make them linen breeches to cover their nakedness; from the loin even unto the thighs they shall reach: And they shall be upon Aaron, and upon his sons, when they come in unto the tabernacle of the congregation, or when they come near unto the altar to minister in the holy place; that they bear not iniquity, and die: it shall be a statute forever unto him and his seed after him. Exodus 28:40-43*

Week 12   Day 2

God said you would become a vessel of honor meet for the master's use, set apart and prepared for every good work. But what does it cost to be a vessel of honor? The **Cost is Consecration - giving all of you for His use.** Everything that God chooses, He consecrates or separates for His, purpose. God also makes sure He covers, protects and guides them. Then He allows you to minister to Him in the sanctuary. He allows you to minister in the sanctuary. God, Himself, ushers you into worship and that is where the presence is created for Him to speak.

Prayer Focus: What has God promised you? What promise did He impress upon you? Listen prayerfully to God in this time of quietness. Write down the truth that He is speaking regarding the dimension He is now calling you to.

57

What Price Are You Willing To Pay?

And the LORD spake unto Moses, saying, Speak unto Aaron and unto his sons, saying, On this wise ye shall bless the children of Israel, saying unto them, The LORD bless thee, and keep thee: The LORD make his face shine upon thee, and be gracious unto thee: The LORD lift up his countenance upon thee, and give thee peace. And they shall put my name upon the children of Israel; and I will bless them. Numbers 6:23-27

Week 12   **Day 3**

_____

_____

_____

_____

_____

_____

_____

_____

_____

_____

_____

Prayer Focus: What is it that I am not seeing that would put me in a better place with you, Lord? Listen to the many ways that God will speak to you in order to make you see what He had hid that was only for you. "Whatever the cost God show me myself that I may give you all"?

_____

_____

_____

_____

_____

_____

_____

_____

_____

_____

_____

_____

If you know anything about God, He plans to compensate, anoint and heal anyone that works for him. God is merely asking you to give your all in exchange for His. To give your all is no more than to consecrate yourself for the glory that lies ahead. Have you never heard that, "suffering of this present time are worthy to be compared to glory that shall be revealed in us" Romans 8:18. The word consecrate means "to be set apart" or "to be holy": of Aaron and his sons (Exodus 28:3, 30:30; the Revised Version (British and American) "sanctify"). The silver and gold and brass and iron of the banned city of Jericho are "consecrated" things (the Revised Version (British and American) "holy") unto the Lord (Joshua 6:19); of the priests (2 Chronicles 26:18); of sacrifices (2 Chronicles 29:33,31:6,Ezra 3:5). Now He has consecrated you!

What Price Are You Willing To Pay?

To this end was I born, and for this cause came I into the world, that I should bear witness unto the truth. Every one that is of the truth heareth my voice. John 18:37

Week 12   Day 4

In suffering, your soul would desire a different way than the way God would have you to go. If you can understand the process of decision making, you will never again go after something that God does not want you to have. **Every decision that you make has either a promise or a penalty attached to it.** First, the enemy will trick you into thinking that there is no penalty for disobedience. Genesis 3:4 says, "And the serpent said unto the woman, **Ye shall not surely die.**" The devil convinced Eve that there would be no pain or suffering if she chose to sin. Second, the enemy will show you how pleasant it is, so you will go after it. Eve saw that the tree was good for food and "pleasant to the eye." Third, the enemy plants desire, "it was a tree to be desired". Once desire has come into your heart, you take hold of it. What do you desire to go after that God does not want you to have? You must now check what is in your heart to make sure that what you desire is coming from the Lord.

Prayer Focus: Promise or Penalty, what will it be for you! What do you choose in times of challenge? Do you have a price? In times of consecration, it is always the will of the Lord that you ought to choose. Search our hearts oh God and if you find anything that prevents us from committing, take it out.

59

What Price Are You Willing To Pay?

This then is the message which we have heard of him, and declare unto you, that God is light, and in him is no darkness at all. 1 John 1:

Week 12 **Day 5**

_____
_____
_____
_____
_____
_____
_____
_____
_____
_____
_____

Prayer Focus: *Master meditating on the Word and being quiet before Him. God teach us how to lay down before you and listen to your heart beat - yielding every one of our member as instruments of service to you.*

_____
_____
_____
_____
_____
_____
_____
_____
_____
_____
_____
_____
_____
_____
_____

Overwhelming desire causes you to break your vow to God every time. How can you identify incorrect desires? Figure out what made you believe that your desire(s) are good! What caused your desire? Desire is in the heart and not in the eyes! However, your eyes will create an image for you and put that image in your heart, and then you start desiring what you do not need. Some of the things that we desire are shown to us on television. Satan's job is to give you vision for what you do not need and derail you from purpose. He may also show seductive scenes from a movie so that you will call "pay for view" and order a particular movie. What you saw created desire in your heart that made you pay for something that you really should not see. **That is only the beginning! The Devil has a plan! But God has a greater plan! In this consecration you are charged by God to walk in the light as He is in the light.**

60

Submit and Obey

And it came to pass, when Moses held up his hand, that Israel prevailed: and when he let down his hand, Amalek prevailed. But Moses 'hands were heavy; and they took a stone, and put it under him, and he sat thereon; and Aaron and Hur stayed p his hands, the one on the one side, and the other on the other side; and his hands were steady until the going down of the s=un. And Joshua discomfited Amalek and his people with the edge of the sword. And the Lord said unto Moses, Write this for a memorial in a book, and re-hearse it in the ears of Joshua: Exodus 17:11-14

Week 13   Day 1 _____

It is the will of God that you become what He desires that you become. Why do you think that some of us fail to become? Has a tadpole, which was born a tadpole, ever set its will to not become a frog? Has a caterpillar, which was born a caterpillar, ever set its will to not become a butterfly? Absolutely not! Neither of these creatures had a choice in their metamorphosis process. You, on the other hand, do. You must realize that you are the only one that was created in the image and the likeness of God. No other creature on the planet has been so privileged. You have been given a will that you can set to submit to the plan of God or to fight against the plan of God. What do you choose? Let's choose to go with God no matter what it costs!

Prayer Focus: What is causing you not to desire what God wants you to do? If you desire what God wants and what is your reasoning for wanting to do it? Is it because you love him and have grown to desire what He want?. Ask God this: Are my motives pleasing to you God because I am wanting to come closer to you?

61

Submit and Obey

Good understanding giveth favor; But the way of the transgressor is hard. Every prudent man worketh with knowledge; But a fool flaunteth his folly. A wicked messenger falleth into evil; But a faithful ambassador is health. Proverbs 13:15-17

Week 13 **Day 2**

_____
_____
_____
_____
_____
_____
_____
_____
_____
_____
_____
_____

Prayer Focus: *Until the pain of staying the same becomes greater than the pain to change, you won't. There is a pain associated with change and there is a pain associated with staying the same. Which pain do you prefer? The pain that ends or the pain that is everlasting? God help us to change even though the pain seems too hard to bare.*

_____
_____
_____
_____
_____
_____
_____
_____
_____
_____
_____
_____

You make the decision to become. The road to becoming is very painful. Conversely, the road to resistance is even more painful. The road to becoming is laden with benefits. The road to resistance is laden with penalties. Pain is inevitable, but the pain that you prefer is your decision alone. Make the right choice. The choice to become is left totally in your hands. The process of metamorphosis is designed to develop you into what is in the mind of God, as it concerns you. If you yield to the process, the pain will prove to be worthwhile, and becoming what God has destined you to be will be unavoidable. If you resist the process, the pain will prove to be unbearable and unnecessary, and what God has destined you to be will follow you to your grave. The real question is will you die and experience death, or will you die and experience life? The choice is yours.

Submit and Obey

And it came to pass, when Moses held up his hand, that Israel prevailed: and when he let down his hand, Amalek prevailed. But Moses 'hands were heavy; and they took a stone, and put it under him, and he sat thereon; and Aaron and Hur stayed p his hands, the one on the one side, and the other on the other side; and his hands were steady until the going down of the s=un. And Joshua discomfited Amalek and his people with the edge of the sword. And the Lord said unto Moses, Write this for a memorial in a book, and rehearse it in the ears of Joshua: Exodus 17:11-14

Week 13   Day 3

The Responsibility Component of Becoming

Nobody just becomes. There are always conditions and processes. These conditions and processes affect our hearing. Genesis 18, which details the patriarch Abraham and his angelic encounter, gives us a great outline of the responsibility component of one that desires his hearing to be complete and effective. Let us review some of the responsibilities: submission, obedience, and reciprocity.

Submission: "And he lift up his eyes and looked, and lo, three men stood by him: and when he saw them, he ran to meet them from the tent door, and bowed himself toward the ground." Genesis 18:2 As Abraham bowed himself to the ground, he placed himself at the disposal of the angels, showing that he had no defense. He was in a posture of total submission. In order to have a successful encounter with the one that would help you become. If you will ever have a sense of becoming, you must find yourself frequently revisiting the place of submission.

Prayer Focus: Check yourself, and ask yourself if there is anything you should be concerned about? God am I still focused on my own vision or am I really submitted to the one you have given me that will help me to become? Am I submitted enough? God what can I do to make my pastor's job easier knowing that my becoming is related to his assignment to the bride of Christ?

63

Submit and Obey

Draw nigh to God, and he will draw nigh to you. Cleanse your hands, ye sinners; and purify your hearts, ye double minded. Be afflicted, and mourn, and weep: let your laughter be turned to mourning, and your joy to heaviness. Humble yourselves in the sight of the Lord, and he shall lift you up. James 4:8-10

Week 13   **Day 4**

_____
_____
_____
_____
_____
_____
_____
_____
_____
_____
_____

Prayer Focus: Father what part of my thinking is holding me up from a closer walk with you? Submission and obedience not applied equals access denied.

_____
_____
_____
_____
_____
_____
_____
_____
_____
_____
_____
_____
_____
_____
_____

Obedience: Your ability to hear God clearer is dependent on your consistency in obeying. How serious are you about obeying God? How quickly do you move to obey what God says and in the direction he gives? **"And I will fetch a morsel of bread, and comfort ye your hearts; after that ye shall pass on: for therefore are you come to your servant. And they said, So do, as thou hast said. And Abraham hastened..." Genesis 18:5-6** After declaring what he would do, the angels commanded him to do as he said. If you continue reading on, you will notice that Abraham **hastened.** Not only was Abraham obedient, he was quick to be obedient. You must hasten to be obedient. If you believe, that you must analyze and critique every command that your leader gives, perhaps hearing ability and its fruit are not for you— and being an illegitimate son/daughter is. You have to swiftly obey God and your leader.

Submit and Obey

Be not deceived; God is not mocked: for whatsoever a man soweth, that shall he also reap. For he that soweth to his flesh shall of the flesh reap corruption; but he that soweth to the Spirit shall of the Spirit reap life everlasting. Galatians 6:7-8

Week 13　　　**Day 5**

_____

_____

_____

Reciprocity is the blessing that comes on one that swiftly obeys "And they said unto him, Where is Sarah thy wife? And he said, Behold, in the tent. And he said, I will certainly return unto thee according to the time of life; and lo, Sarah thy wife shall have a son..." Genesis 18:9-10 How is it that reciprocity is considered to be a man or woman of God's responsibility and privilege? In the first eight verses of this chapter, Abraham is found serving until his heart's content. Abraham ran to meet the angels from the tent door, fetched their water, washed their feet, fetched them bread, fetched a tender calf for them and provided the angels with a tasty meal underneath the tree. What a servant! Now, Abraham's hour of reciprocity was nigh. It was his responsibility and privilege to be in place in order to receive the reciprocal blessing. As men and women of God, each of your blessings have been addressed to

_____

_____

_____

_____

_____

_____

_____

_____

_____

_____

_____

Prayer Focus: *Seek God about your destiny and do an evaluation on where you laid your seed. What type of seed did you leave at the last ministry or church that you attended? What type of seed are you leaving where you are now? What is God saying? Do you need to dig up some seed or call crop failure to some? Are you able to fertilize what you've already planted?*

_____

_____

_____

_____

_____

_____

_____

_____

_____

_____

_____

Push Past The Pressure

Now the just shall live by faith: but if any man draw back, my soul shall have no pleasure in him. But we are not of them who draw back unto perdition; but of them that believe to the saving of the soul. Hebrews 10:38-39

Week 14   **Day 1**

_____

_____

_____

_____

_____

_____

_____

_____

_____

_____

_____

_____

Prayer Focus: Ask God to help you get past this time of wanting to quit. Go after God with all that is within you. God will give you steps to take out any level of depression. What is God saying to do in order to get out of this dilemma? Does what you heard match what the bible says? God will never speak contrary to His Word (the Bible)..

_____

_____

_____

_____

_____

_____

_____

_____

_____

_____

_____

_____

_____

_____

Has the pressure increased yet? Are you about ready to quit? You have only begun. God is nowhere near done yet. You must come to the persuasion that it is not a matter of quitting. The question is, how do you accomplish the next assignment? Regardless of the pressure, you cannot quit. Quitting registers in the mind of God as a postponement, not the end of the assignment. I understand when you quit it is because you feel you are out of answers, but that is exactly where God wants you. When you feel you are out of answers, then God can jump in and give you answers you do did not know existed. God loves it when we run out of road because it at that place, He can begin

Push Past The Pressure

And when the devil had ended all the temptation, he departed from him for a season. And Jesus returned in the power of the Spirit into Galilee: and there went out a fame of him through all the region round about. Luke 4:13-4

Week 14   Day 2

Has the pressure increased yet? Are you about ready to quit? There is a tremendous measure of power that will show up when you endure the test of quitting. Jesus came down out of the wilderness in the power of the Spirit once He endured the test. There is a powerful release of the anointing if you can just get through the test. What most people don't understand is you hear God so much clearer when you endure tests you must take. Somewhere along the way, your mind must check out so the mind of Christ will work.

Prayer Focus: If you have thought about quitting, make a quality decision now against quitting and repent. Then make another decision to stand and having done all to keep on standing. Then watch God show up on and speak up. Did you notice when Jesus was going through the wilderness, God never spoke nor sent angels to minister to him until he endured the test? This is your time to commit and submit to the will of God.

Push Past The Pressure

Now the just shall live by faith: but if any man draw back, my soul shall have no pleasure in him. But we are not of them who draw back unto perdition; but of them that believe to the saving of the soul. Hebrews 10:38-39

Week 14   **Day 3**

_____

_____

_____

_____

_____

_____

_____

_____

_____

_____

_____

Has the pressure increased yet? Are you about ready to quit? God will make the necessary deposit in you, if you don't draw back. God's word says, "He is not of them that draw back." If we could only get to the place where we will be determined to finish our course, then God will speak up and show up in a big way. God is waiting on you to make a declaration of faith that you will not lose heart, faint or run off.

Prayer Focus: Deal with the areas in your life where you have drawn away from the real intent of God. Deal with the frailties in your life that seem to prevent you from fulfilling your God given purpose..

_____

_____

_____

_____

_____

_____

_____

_____

_____

_____

_____

_____

_____

_____

Push Past The Pressure

Save that the Holy Ghost witnesseth in every city, saying that bonds and afflictions abide me.But none of these things move me, neither count I my life dear unto myself, so that I might finish my course with joy, and the ministry, which I have received of the Lord Jesus, to testify the gospel of the grace of God. Acts 20:23-24

Week 14   Day 4

Are you about still ready to quit? Evaluate to what extent you have suffered. I believe you will come to the conclusion that what you have gone through up to this point has not yet measured up to what some others around you have gone through. At this stage in your life, I think you can conclude that you are grateful that you are where you are. Just look back at how far you have come. Well, that is the thing Satan does not does not want you to do. He knows that if you just look back a little to observe how far you have come and the level of growth you have obtained, encouragement will hit your heart and you will never give up. These are the things that causes you to listen deeply and it is at those times you hear God best.

Prayer Focus: Ask God if you were honest enough on yesterday about your commitment. If you were not honest enough, then increase your commitment. Then you too can say with Paul, "none of these things move me neither count I my life dear unto myself that I might finish my course with joy." It is this kind of commitment that drives you towards intimacy.

Push Past The Pressure

Whereupon, O king Agrippa, I was not disobedient unto the heavenly vision:
Acts 26:19

_____

_____

_____

_____

_____

_____

_____

_____

_____

_____

_____

Prayer Focus: Return to worship and declare that God is good and that He is worthy to be praised. Take the rest of your time and worship God and watch his presence so fill the room where you are.

_____

_____

_____

_____

_____

_____

_____

_____

_____

_____

_____

_____

_____

Week 14   Day 5

You should be able to come to a place of worship now that you have settled the differences between you and God - now that you know God is with you and not against you. God was only desiring you to push past the pressure you were going through so that you could break free from the distractions and come into the glorious liberty of His Word. Now come to a place of worship and thanksgiving before God and say to those around you as Paul said to King Agrippa, **"I was not disobedient to the heavenly vision"** nor was I disobedient to the word I heard impressed in my spirit.

Guarding Your Anointing

The Lord called Samuel: and he answered, Here am I. And he ran unto Eli, and said, Here am I; for thou calledst me. And he said, I called not; lie down again. And he went and lay down. And the Lord called yet again, Samuel.and Samuel arose went to Eli, and said, Here am I; for thou didst call me. And he answered, I called not, my son; lie down again. 1Samuel 3:4-6

Week 15   Day 1 _____

There is an assault on the anointing on the body of Christ and you must protect it with everything that you have. You as men/women of God should rise up with the pureness of God coming out of our heart every day, so that everything that you say surely comes to pass. Sometimes you are greatly hindered because you don't who you are. It has not yet clicked in your thinking that "now are we the sons of God and it doth not yet appear what we shall be, but we when he appears we shall be like him." Yes, with or without a call to ministry, "now are you a child of God" and you have the anointing of God on you. You have to become a voice in the area where you live. God would love to speak to you and share things with you He cannot say to another. People should be looking for a word from God from your mouth. They should be able to say there is a man of God or a woman of God in this city. God will prepare you with a word in your private time as you worship in His presence and wait quietly before Him. The anointing is what endues you with ability to do, hear and say what many other can't. Who are you? A child of the living of God in you. Guard it with your life.

Prayer Focus: Return to worship and declare the goodness of God! In your morning announce that He is worthy to be praised. Ask God to show you how to enter His rest so that you can experience the rest of God. There is so much more of Him that you have not yet seen.

Guarding Your Anointing

And the Lord came, and stood, and called as at other times, Samuel, Samuel. Then Samuel answered, Speak; for thy servant heareth. And the Lord said to Samuel, Behold, I will do a thing in Israel, at which both the ears of every one that heareth it shall tingle. 1 Samuel 3:10-11

Week 15 **Day 2**

_____

_____

_____

_____

_____

_____

_____

_____

_____

_____

_____

Prayer Focus: As you return to worship this morning, will you set your will to listen? God will only speak if He knows you are listening. Remember, you have to set your will to hear. Listening is a learned skill. It does not automatically come.

_____

_____

_____

_____

_____

_____

_____

_____

_____

_____

_____

_____

_____

There is an anointing that rests on you to do what God has assigned to you in a particular season and for a certain reason. But you have walked in your own way and have not understood that there is an anointing that is on you. Your mindset may be to question why God would want to use you and you have let the anointing that is on your life lay dormant. It is difficult to see the will of God if you have never left the position of your own will. God desires to share His will with you and in doing so, He is literally sharing His heart. Do not miss this opportunity to see the heart of God in your situation. When God decided to destroy Sodom and Gomorra, He found His friend Abraham and opened His heart to him. Will you set your will aside that you might hear the plans of our Holy God? Those plans may involve your life or a love one.

Guarding Your Anointing

And the Lord came, and stood, and called as at other times, Samuel, Samuel. Then Samuel answered, Speak; for thy servant heareth. And the Lord said to Samuel, Behold, I will do a thing in Israel, at which both the ears of every one that heareth it shall tingle. 1 Samuel 3:10-11

Week 15   Day 3

You are Anointed for a Reason and a Season

There is an anointing on you and in you for a specific reason. It is in you so that you will be able to come to the highest height in God that your flesh will allow. Your flesh will prevent you from reaching the height of your anointing. The anointing that is upon you a shifts. It is on you for one assignment in this season, but it shifts to another assignment in the next season. The anointing on you is specifically tailored to your assignment. There is a link between what your assignment is and the anointing that rests on you. You must understand what is on us in a particular season and why it is there. Samuel had an anointing on him that was there before he ever realized that God had had selected him as a prophet for his nation. God is speaking to you because He is getting you ready for something you are not ready for right now. God trained little Samuel to hear before he even knew that God wanted to talk to him. The anointing was there and so was the willingness, but hearing God was far from his thinking. One of the links to your hearing is the person that God has put over your life: your pastor, mentor and/or spiritual father. Who is the Eli in your life that trains you to hear or tells you when you have heard God at the next level? The voice you hear may sound like the one that is called to train you.

Prayer Focus: Create a level of sensitivity in your life. Are you prepared to hear from God? At this stage in your relationship, you should have developed a life of praise, worship, truth, love and joy. You should also know how to deeply listen for the voice of God.

73

Guarding Your Anointing

And the Lord said to Samuel, Behold, I will do a thing in Israel, at which both the ears of every one that heareth it shall tingle. 1 Samuel 3:11

_____
_____
_____
_____
_____
_____
_____
_____
_____
_____
_____
_____

Prayer Focus: What is God saying to you that you may be missing? There are so many times that God says something to you and you think that it was you and not God. By now, you are being challenged in your hearing. God is really saying something; what is he saying?

_____
_____
_____
_____
_____
_____
_____
_____
_____
_____
_____
_____
_____
_____
_____
_____
_____

The anointing and the ability to hear God is not just on your pastor, set gift, or your man or woman of God. If you walk close enough to him/her, that same anointing and ability to hear rolls down on you. You cannot go into a room where there is an aroma, and that aroma does not get on you. You cannot gain access to a person and they keep their things from you. No matter how much perfume or cologne you put on in the morning; when you walk into a 7- Eleven about 7AM, there is an aroma of coffee that will be on you when you leave out of the store; even if you have not gone near the coffee. If a natural product like coffee can linger on you, if you stay under your man/woman of God, the anointing on them comes down on you. The ultimate anointing that you experience actually rest on your man/woman of God. He/she has an anointing to preach, teach, usher, sing, play music, clean the floor, wash walls, clean toilets, change light bulbs, produce books, whatever needs to be done. But since he/she cannot not do all of that and still do what God told them to do, they pass that anointing off to you. What they pass to you is a link to a greater anointing or ability. This is the power of access. Samuel walked close with Eli and gained access to his ability to hear God. If you measure the distance between you and your shepherd, how close would you say you are to their ability?

Guarding Your Anointing

And Samuel told him every whit, and hid nothing from him. And he said, It is the Lord: let him do what seemeth him good. And Samuel grew, and the Lord was with him, and did let none of his words fall to the ground. And all Israel from Dan even to Beersheba knew that Samuel was established to be a prophet of the Lord. And the Lord appeared again in Shiloh: for the Lord revealed himself to Samuel in Shiloh by the word of the Lord. 1 Samuel 3:18-21

Week 15   Day 5

Seeing, hearing and speaking are in the head and the working is in the body. However, in these days God is calling the whole body to function and therefore, He is giving the body access if you are willing and apply yourself. You need to stay hidden under your authority, close enough where you can hear their heart beat until it is time to be sent out. There are times when it seems hard to stay under authority and even close to it, because it seems like authority wants to hurt and deprive you. But, God has set you under authority so they can protect you. When you perfect your hearing and learn to live in your secret place, room is made for you to come out. The Bible says in **Proverbs 18:16, "A man's gift maketh room for him, and bringeth him before great men."** Your gift makes room for you. The skill of listening creates doors for you. There is an anointing on your life and if the Devil ever gets a glimpse of your anointing, he will send an Athaliah after you to make sure that you make all of the wrong decisions. Joash was hidden for six years and in the seventh year, he was sent forth. At seven years old, Athaliah sees the king's son and realizes that her government has been overthrown. Athaliah cried, "Treason, treason!" In other words, you have deceived me.

Prayer Focus: Seek God with your whole heart. Ask God what problem(s) you are anointed to solve? Wait for the answer on that special note in your secret place.

75

Worship, An Act Of Your Will

There is therefore now no condemnation to them which are in Christ Jesus, who walk not after the flesh, but after the Spirit. For the law of the Spirit of life in Christ Jesus hath made me free from the law of sin and death. For what the law could not do, in that it was weak through the flesh, God sending his own Son in the likeness of sinful flesh, and for sin, condemned sin in the flesh:
Romans 8:1-3

Week 16　　　　　**Day 1**

_____

_____

_____

_____

_____

_____

_____

_____

_____

_____

_____

_____

*Prayer Focus: Prepare your heart for this a lifestyle of worship. Jesus prepared the **woman at the well** for a lifestyle of worship. Now you must prepare for worship. What effort are you making to come and worship at his feet? Remember these things as you enter into the presence God:*

1. ***Prepare your heart for Worship***
2. *Prepare a time for Worship*
3. *Prepare a place for Worship*

Now let's enter in with the Lord and see what He will say today.

As we begin to think about coming into another level of hearing God, you have to think about the level of worship you operate in. Worship is your communion with the Lord. Worship illustrates your willingness you to come into God's presence. **"Worship means to fall down, bow down to, show reverence to, respectfully welcome. It means to serve. It also means give as in an offering."** When you give that is also a form of worship as far as God is concerned. The best way to explain worship as a life style to you is to get your focus of the cross or the tabernacle, which is the same pattern. Real worship requires the alignment of your lips, your mouth and your heart offering fruit unto God.

_____

_____

_____

_____

_____

_____

_____

_____

_____

_____

Worship, An Act Of Your Will

And Abraham said, My son, God will provide himself a lamb for a burnt offering: so they went both of them together. And they came to the place which God had told him of; and Abraham built an altar there, and laid the wood in order, and bound Isaac his son, and laid him on the altar upon the wood. And Abraham stretched forth his hand, and took the knife to slay his son. Genesis 22:8-10

Week 16   Day 2

How you worship is by God's design. And as you think about worshiping according to God's design, you have to include the sacrifice component of the Tabernacle as they stood before the Brazen Altar. Here you stand at the Outer Court of your life, and God requires a sacrifice from you before you step into the next place in Him to be washed at the Brazen Laver. God is requiring a sacrifice from you. What will you give Him seeing that His sacrifice for you was His son? Micah says, **"He has shown thee oh man what is good and what doeth the Lord require of thee, to love mercy, do justly and walk humbly with thy God."** Micah 6:8 That, my friend, is a self-sacrifice. God is looking for you and me to be the sacrifice, even a living sacrifice. It is good to give things and sometimes it is even better to give money, but what God considers to be most valuable is your life as a living sacrifice. Now is a good time to bring yourself to the brazen altar.

<u>Brazen Altar:</u> This is the place to lay down all of your Sin (flesh). If your sins are not removed, then your heart is not clear for the worship of God to come in. For that reason God says in His word, **1John 1:9** Jesus paid the Price here at the foot of the cross.

Prayer Focus: In your time with God this morning ask; "How do I give all that I am?" Wait for the answer as He takes His time to answer.

77

Worship, An Act Of Your Will

There is therefore now no condemnation to them which are in Christ Jesus, who walk not after the flesh, but after the Spirit. For the law of the Spirit of life in Christ Jesus hath made me free from the law of sin and death. For what the law could not do, in that it was weak through the flesh, God sending his own Son in the likeness of sinful flesh, and for sin, condemned sin in the flesh:
Romans 8:1-3

_____

_____

_____

_____

_____

_____

_____

_____

_____

_____

_____

Week 16   Day 3

The Brazen Laver is the place to be washed from all your past sins now that you have sacrificed yourself at the Brazen (Flesh) Altar. **How many times have you come by the place of sacrifice and never realized the need for being washed from all the sin that was once on you?** The washing is just as important as the sacrifice. Jesus said, "Now you are clean through the word I have spoken to you." What Jesus said affects the conscience level of the cleansing you realize. How can you have faith in that you have not heard seeing that **"faith cometh by hearing?"** As you embrace the idea of the Tabernacle setting and what it represents, let the word cleanse and wash you thoroughly as you step into this next season. The **Brazen Laver: (Brass symbolic of Flesh)** is a bowl for washing. Remember (out of Jesus' side flowed blood and water). This is the place where you make sure you are clean before you ever enter in the Holy Place.

Prayer Focus: Let this morning be a morning of cleansing. Do this by meditating on the Word and letting the Word you meditate on sink deep in your heart. Pray and ask God what scripture to meditate on as He washes you from past guilt. According to God's Word, "there is therefore now no condemnation to them that are in Christ Jesus.

_____

_____

_____

_____

_____

_____

_____

_____

_____

_____

_____

_____

Worship, An Act Of Your Will

For I have received of the Lord that which also I delivered unto you, That the Lord Jesus the same night in which he was betrayed took bread: And when he had given thanks, he brake it, and said, Take, eat: this is my body, which is broken for you: this do in remembrance of me. After the same manner also he took the cup, when he had supped, saying, This cup is the new testament in my blood: this do ye, as oft as ye drink it, in remembrance of me. For as often as ye eat this bread, and drink this cup, ye do shew the Lord's death till he come.
1 Corinthians 11:25-26

Week 16   Day 4

Enter the Holy Place this morning, where you will have fellowship with God the Father at the first level of His presence. When you enter, it is imperative that you have a sense of awe when you see the Gold that represents the presence of God. The candlestick in the book of Revelation represents the Church. Therefore, if you take the candlestick **(L)** out of the word GOLD, you end up with God alone. But when you put the candlestick **(L)** back in the word Gold, you have the Church back in fellowship with God. You are like Gold tried in the fire when you start pushing on purpose through the pressure. But if you stop, you have just taken the **(L)** out of the word Gold. Gold that is not tried, very well may not be gold. **Golden Candlesticks: (Gold symbolic of God)**: This is where man must part. The candlesticks were not something that was going to burn candles but, oil. **This is symbolic of you having a continuous supply of oil so that you could give light whenever darkness is around. John 8:12.** You are now ready and able to go to the Communion table with full confidence that you are in God. The Communion table is a place of fellowship.
The Table of Shewbread: This table represents Jesus in His administration (service) to the Church. This next place is not accessible if you can't spread toward the Church and the world with light and services. Shewbread also speaks of the body of the Lord and holy communion. Matthew 26:26-28 The shewbread is the communion of the Lord that is broken for you.

Prayer Focus: *Honor of the Word brings on power from the Word. Whatever word God will have you to speak, He wants it honored. But who will honor a word that comes from a vessel that has not been purified? Spend some time today correcting the impure thoughts you think that makes your words impure. The impure thoughts come from an impure heart. And nothing can purify the heart like a fiery trial.*

Worship, An Act Of Your Will

Having therefore, brethren, boldness to enter into the holiest by the blood of Jesus, By a new and living way, which he hath consecrated for us, through the veil, that is to say, his flesh; And having an high priest over the house of God; Let us draw near with a true heart in full assurance of faith, having our hearts sprinkled from an evil conscience, and our bodies washed with pure water.
Hebrews 10:19-22

Week 16   **Day 5**

_____

_____

_____

_____

_____

_____

_____

_____

_____

_____

_____

Prayer Focus: Let this morning be a time of Worship! Worship God for what you know God is desiring from you. If you believe that God is in you, then you must fight to enter this place. This is not a day to easily quit. Enter In!

_____

_____

_____

_____

_____

_____

_____

_____

_____

_____

_____

_____

_____

_____

Intimacy is the ultimate place you should desire to enter while you are in the earth. It is the place of ultimate sacrificing of self, where you are able to come into the presence of God without guilt or shame. There is no more you - just God. This is the place you bow down without pretense, just in awe of God's glory because that is the part of Him that He shares with you. It is at this point that you can truly say, "I am Yielding My Best For His Glory. God I present all of me to you."

The Altar of Incense: It always speaks of prayer and intercession in this intimate place with God. All you have seen so far creates a lifestyle of worship and smells like sweet incense in the nostrils of God. Many times one wants to enter the heights of worship without ever first coming to the place of total surrender. It takes a made up mind and a yielded heart to get up in the morning. When you do come to this place, God sees it as worship to Him; but it is not the height of worship.

The Veil or Covering: This second veil was symbolic of that which covers the glory. The thickness of glory is not seen or experienced by everyone; just those that have been able to press through life's circumstances beyond the second veil into the Holy of Holies.

It is Finished

Therefore seeing we have this ministry, as we have received mercy, we faint not; 2 But have renounced the hidden things of dishonesty, not walking in craftiness, nor handling the word of God deceitfully; but by manifestation of the truth1 Corinthians 11:25-26

Week 17   Day 1

As you continue in this intimate place, it is very important to remember that this is a time of stripping off all the unseen things that could hinder what God is doing and desiring to do in your life. Even though you have completely given yourself over to God and you are completely yielding yourself to Him, there are things that are hidden in your life that have been there for a while. The only way to really get to those things is to get them to show themselves and that happens through your fasting while on this consecration. What that means is you must come before God "Naked and Not Ashamed". Everything does not come up at once. It comes up one by one, and challenge by challenge. Your job is to not get discouraged, but to kill each one as they show themselves. Things showing up does not mean you have not arrived at this intimate place, it just means your position with God is being challenged. Why would Satan want to run you out of your intimate place if he knows that God has released you in that place? Was it not in that intimate place when Satan tried to run Jesus out and make him abort His destiny? Then, Satan will try you also. The real test is can or will you **"continue in my word THEN are my disciples indeed."** If you don't, Satan gets to try you as one that is not righteous.

Prayer Focus: *Find out what tries to interfere with your level of consecration and get it out of your life. Do you need your commitment strengthened at this point in life? Pray "our Father which art in heaven hallowed be thy name, thy kingdom come thy will be done in earth as it is in heaven..." Matthew 6: 9-10*

81

It is Finished

And they were both naked, the man and his wife, and were not ashamed.
Genesis 2:2

_____

_____

_____

_____

_____

_____

_____

_____

_____

_____

_____

_____

_____

Prayer Focus: Ask yourself, "Have I made a quality decision to get things out of my life that are not necessarily sin, but are not helpful to God's purpose in my life?" In this season we are preparing God's people for unhindered worship that brings Manifested Glory for a new dimension. Are you positioned to help anyone? Can you be transparent enough to convince them to come out from where they are? Are You Naked and Not Ashamed?

_____

_____

_____

_____

_____

_____

_____

_____

_____

_____

_____

Week 17   Day 2

In these time you will find yourselves needing to shift in your thinking from one dimension, moving progressively through the second dimension and advancing into the third dimension of (supernatural thinking). How will you accomplish that? You will accomplish shifting from dimension to dimension by changing the way you think. Paul says in the book of Philippians, **"let this mind be in you which was also in Christ Jesus."** Proverbs says, **"as a man thinks in his heart so is he."** I find that when you do not change in your thought process, God has to find a way to strip you down until you are "Naked and Not Ashamed" and that normally takes some time to do.

Your thinking controls your production and position. People with third-dimensional thinking believe they can accomplish what seems to be impossible realizing "it is God in me He does the work." One of the things I have found is in order to accomplish what seems impossible, you have to think and believe beyond the norm. The Word of God says things like, **"If ye then be risen with Christ seek those things which are above where Christ sitteth at the right hand of God, Set your affections on things above not on things in the earth."** I am talking about living where Jesus lived (in the supernatural), where all things are possible. The two main things you have to have in order to live in that kind of place is: nothing hidden (Naked) and being free of condemnation (Ashamed).

It is Finished

Therefore seeing we have this ministry, as we have received mercy, we faint not; 2 But have renounced the hidden things of dishonesty, not walking in craftiness, nor handling the word of God deceitfully; but by manifestation of the truth commending ourselves to every man's conscience in the sight of God.
1 Corinthians 4:1-2

Week 17   Day 3 _____

There are time you may seem to be filled with shame and pride because of where you have been in your life. I don't think you realize that hiding things, instead of repenting makes things worst. Therefore, God pushes you to renounce the hidden things of dishonesty. Renounce the hidden things of dishonesty, acknowledge that those things are there in your life and start a process of getting rid of them by abandoning them. One thing you must be certain of is if you abandon something, more than likely you will be drawn to something else. Therefore, as you renounce or abandon the hidden things in your life, draw near to God with all your heart. Set your affections on things above where Christ is seated. What things? The kind of intimacy Jesus described as having with the Father; things like when Jesus would say, **"Father, you always hear me when I pray"** or **"I only do what I have seen of my Father."** This is the kind of intimacy God desires to have with you as you renounce the hidden things of dishonesty and become naked and not ashamed.

Prayer Focus: God, do I need to change the position which I mentally embrace? Am I following you close enough to make this kind of change? Are we not close enough? Seek God with pure heart.

83

It is Finished

There is therefore now no condemnation to them which are in Christ Jesus, who walk not after the flesh, but after the Spirit. Romans 8:1

Week 17   Day 4

Are you experiencing the peace that comes with having a pure conscience? Now that you have emptied out your hidden secrets to the Father and have stepped into the light of Jesus, you can also embrace what comes with doing so. There are times that you remember those things you have previously renounced, but that is not you nor is it the Father bringing those things back to your remembrance. When the past is bought into your future, it is orchestrated by the Devil. Your conscience is clean of such things. Then why are you still thinking about what has past? The book of Revelation calls Satan the accuser of the brethren and unfortunately, there are Christians that have decided to work with Satan to keep you reminded of your past. Then how do you address those accusations? You don't! If your conscience is clear, you recall those things on purpose. **There is therefore now no condemnation to those that are in Christ Jesus.** You are in Christ and that means you: therefore, should have peace on purpose.

Prayer Focus: *God has cleared you of all guilt! If there is a remembrance of your past, bow down now and give it to Jesus! You are not condemned; you are forgiven. Therefore, what is God saying that He will amazingly perform in your tomorrow? Listen with your clean conscience.*

84

It is Finished

Blotting out the handwriting of ordinances that was against us, which was contrary to us, and took it out of the way, nailing it to his cross; And having spoiled principalities and powers, he made a shew of them openly, triumphing over them in it. Colossians 2:14-15

Week 17   Day 5

On the day that Jesus was on the cross one of the things Jesus said was, **"It is finished."** I often wondered what He meant by those words and I am sure you did also. As you have prayed this week and meditated on what God has been speaking in your spirit, He has been revealing to you that it has been finished in your life as well. Jesus had you in mind as He uttered those words on that cross. Jesus was saying your sins are finished! Your past is finished! Your struggle with life is finished! Your grief is finished! Your sicknesses and diseases are finished! He said it was nailed to the cross, therefore, blotting out everything that was against you and taking it out of the way. Therefore, when Jesus said it was finished, He was affirming that it is all out of your way now. Don't be hindered ever again by that which is in the past.

Prayer Focus: You are new in Christ Jesus! Go and have a clear conscience today knowing you hear better that way.

Receive Your Endowment

Then cometh Jesus with them unto a place called Gethsemane, and saith unto the disciples, Sit ye here, while I go and pray yonder. And he took with him Peter and the two sons of Zebedee, and began to be sorrowful and very heavy. Then saith he unto them, My soul is exceeding sorrowful, even unto death: tarry ye here, and watch with me. And he went a little further, and fell on his face, and prayed, saying, O my Father, if it be possible, let this cup pass from me: nevertheless not as I will, but as thou wilt. Matthew 26:36-39

Week 18　　　　　**Day 1**

There are great things that come from consecration. Much is lost because of the lack of consecration. Consecration has brought increase in this season that many have been unable to tap into. God is certainly looking for vessels that will receive the endowment that is necessary for increase to come in many different areas. Consecration brought Solomon his endowment of wisdom and understanding. It has brought Apostle Paul such revelation as mentioned in **2 Corinthians 12**. So much so that he was able to say, **"I knew a man one day whether in the body or out of the body I cannot tell God knoweth such a one caught up to the third heaven."** Think about it - consecration causes you to see in a different dimension. Peter's consecration led him into the divine nature and out of fleshly thinking. Where will you allow your consecration to lead you? It should lead you into a realm that you have not been nor functioned in before.

Prayer Focus: God what will I need to do to get this next endowment? What have I not given of myself that you are requiring of me? Teach me to wait before you and listen!

Receive Your Endowment

And, behold, I send the promise of my Father upon you: but tarry ye in the city of Jerusalem, until ye be endued with power from on high. Luke 24:49

Week 18   Day 2

There are great things that come from consecration. One of the necessary steps of getting the needed endowment is to stay in a consecrated place/state of being. That means to stay in that protected place called Jerusalem/home, the place of covering. It is at that place and in the right time that God will bring the necessary endowment from Himself and then from that covering. As you are in the place of covering, what are you gleaning from the one who covers you that is usable in your place that God is calling you to? Joshua gleaned from Moses, Elisha from Elijah and Peter from Jesus. In this time of consecration, you have to be gathering something from the one you are sent to. There is something that comes from their sacrifice, their suffering and their service that you are to receive.

Prayer Focus: God, do I need to change the position which I mentally embrace? Am I following you close enough to make this kind of change? Are we not close enough? Seek God with pure heart.

Receive Your Endowment

Then cometh Jesus with them unto a place called Gethsemane, and saith unto the disciples, Sit ye here, while I go and pray yonder. And he took with him Peter and the two sons of Zebedee, and began to be sorrowful and very heavy. Then saith he unto them, My soul is exceeding sorrowful, even unto death: tarry ye here, and watch with me. And he went a little further, and fell on his face, and prayed, saying, O my Father, if it be possible, let this cup pass from me: nevertheless not as I will, but as thou wilt. Matthew 26:36-39

Week 18   **Day 3**

_____

_____

_____

_____

_____

_____

_____

_____

_____

_____

_____

Prayer Focus: God will always appear at the place where He told you to go. Are you there yet? Have you made your move? What is God saying to you regarding that place? What are you expecting to get from that place? It is a place of feeding, yielding and where your gift can be nurtured. There is a promise on the way for your obedience in that place!

_____

_____

_____

_____

_____

_____

_____

_____

_____

There are great things that come from consecration. Much is lost because of the lack of consecration. Consecration has brought increase in this season that many have been unable to tap into. God is certainly looking for vessels that will receive the endowment that is necessary for increase to come in many different areas. Consecration brought Solomon his endowment of wisdom and understanding. It has brought Apostle Paul such revelation as mentioned in **2 Corinthians 12.** So much so that he was able to say, **"I knew a man one day whether in the body or out of the body I cannot tell God knoweth such a one caught up to the third heaven."** Think about it - consecration causes you to see in a different dimension. Peter's consecration led him into the divine nature and out of fleshly thinking. Where will you allow your consecration to lead you? It should lead you into a realm that you have not been nor functioned in before.

Receive Your Endowment

Then cometh Jesus with them unto a place called Gethsemane, and saith unto the disciples, Sit ye here, while I go and pray yonder. And he took with him Peter and the two sons of Zebedee, and began to be sorrowful and very heavy. Then saith he unto them, My soul is exceeding sorrowful, even unto death: tarry ye here, and watch with me. And he went a little further, and fell on his face, and prayed, saying, O my Father, if it be possible, let this cup pass from me: nevertheless not as I will, but as thou wilt. Matthew 26:36-39

Week 18   **Day 4**

There are great things that come from consecration. Promise brings endowment and endowment brings manifestation. This is the hour of promise that God is looking to bring some sense of fulfillment to your life. God is the God of promise and He greatly desires to bring fulfillment and manifestation in your life. God can only do what He desires to do for you if you will throw yourself down before Him completely yielding to God everything you are. This is the place of the dying of the Lord. Jesus died in Gethsemane before He ever really got to the cross. The amazing thing is that He allowed Peter, James and John to see Him die there. You are not dead until you let those closest to you see your vulnerable state. You are considered dead when those that have seen you in your strong days are allowed to see you in your days of consecration where God has squeezed a yes out of you. It is at that time God will really show himself strong in you.

Prayer Focus: There are different types of endowments that God desires to bring in your life. But the main question is, "What type of endowment are you after and what death are you willing to die?" God has what you desire, but He wants you to come after it.

Receive Your Endowment

Because thou hast been my help, therefore in the shadow of thy wings will I rejoice. My soul followeth hard after thee: thy right hand upholdeth me.
Psalms 63:7-8

Week 18   **Day 5**

There are great things that come from consecration. As you think of the place of consecration, promise, fulfillment, and endowment, you must always remember that it costs something. The question is, "Are you willing to pay the price for it?" As we close this time, please remember to go hard after God understanding that it is the only way that true fulfillment can happen. Knowing that God has kept you- even in times when you were not trying to keep yourself. Go hard after El- El yon (The all mighty God). As you go hard after God, remember what Jacob said when he wrestled with the Angel; **"I will not let you go until you bless me."** With that kind of tenacity, God will see your consecration. At a point like that, God will say the same thing that was said to Jacob; **"What is your name?"** And Jacob answers, "Jacob" or deceiver! The Angel says, "Your name shall be called Israel" - meaning prince with God.

Prayer Focus: Seek God's face like it is your last time! The key word in your thoughts should be desperation. What changes are you desperate for? Are you willing to wrestle all night in prayer if need be? Sometimes that is the only answer that makes sense!

90

When God Whispers Your To Capture Your Attention

And the angel of the Lord appeared unto him in a flame of fire out of the midst of a bush: and he looked, and, behold, the bush burned with fire, and the bush was not consumed. 3 And Moses said, I will now turn aside, and see this great sight, why the bush is not burnt. 4 And when the Lord saw that he turned aside to see, God called unto him out of the midst of the bush, and said, Moses, Moses. And he said, Here am I. Exodus 3:2-4

Week 19   Day 1

This scripture sounds like a private call from the Lord to an assignment that is familiar to Moses. Sometimes God just whispers a thing to us as He reminds us of previous assignments and prepares us for future ones. Moses, like us is being drawn to a thing that has captured his attention and reminds him of an assignment he once possessed or will possess. He sees a bush that is burning and is not consumed, as his heart burned with his assignment in a past time when he was in Egypt. The fire he felt burn in him drove him to deliver a Hebrew that was being mistreated. In the bush there was a whisper of God that reminded him of where he was and in the same bush the whisper was telling him where he would be going in the next season. As God speak to you about the things in your life that are calling you to action, understand it is but a whisper.

Prayer Focus: Father, please sensitize my spirit to the leading of the Holy Spirit that I may hear clearly. What is your burning bush that God is speaking out of that is calling you to duty?

91

When God Whispers Your To Capture Your Attention

And the angel of the Lord appeared unto him in a flame of fire out of the midst of a bush: and he looked, and, behold, the bush burned with fire, and the bush was not consumed. 3 And Moses said, I will now turn aside, and see this great sight, why the bush is not burnt. 4 And when the Lord saw that he turned aside to see, God called unto him out of the midst of the bush, and said, Moses, Moses. And he said, Here am I. Exodus 3:2-4

Week 19   **Day 2**

_____

_____

_____

_____

_____

_____

_____

_____

_____

_____

_____

Prayer Focus: Will you now "turn aside to see this bush that is burning that is not consumed? What is God calling you to? God teach me to hear silent sounds that are calling me to purpose? Help me to see my bush that is burning that will not go out.

How do I Identify the things that are calling me to action? I know it is, because it drives me away from natural assignments and pulls me toward things that I am purposed to do in life. Oh the fascination of the God assignment. I, like Moses feel called away time-to-time from what I normally do in order to participate in what seems so normal for me. What is the one thing you are driven to do? What is it that captures your attention more than your favorite meal? What will you lose sleep over at night to do in the morning, noon or evening? That one thing is called your burning bush.

_____

_____

_____

_____

_____

_____

_____

_____

_____

_____

_____

_____

When God Whispers Your To Capture Your Attention

And the angel of the Lord appeared unto him in a flame of fire out of the midst of a bush: and he looked, and, behold, the bush burned with fire, and the bush was not consumed. 3 And Moses said, I will now turn aside, and see this great sight, why the bush is not burnt. 4 And when the Lord saw that he turned aside to see, God called unto him out of the midst of the bush, and said, Moses, Moses. And he said, Here am I. Exodus 3:2-4

Week 19   **Day 3** _____

There is something about when God sees you respond to your sensitivity. God saw Moses turn in obedience to what he was sensing about the bush that was not consumed as it burned. This is the yielding that God was hoping for out of Moses and now God is hoping for this same yielding out of you. God knows if you can hear Him out of the bush that is burning in your life, then undoubtedly you will hear His voice above anything. God also knows if you will yield to a call out of a bush that is burning, then you will also yield to His voice that you hear that is coming from where ever He sends it. There is a clarion call that only you can respond to and that call is for you! Are You Ready?

Prayer Focus: God fill my mouth with all good things. Get your bible out now and meditate on the Word to see what God will have you to pray. As you do so, listen deeply to what God is speaking through to bring you into your next assignment.

93

When God Whispers Your To Capture Your Attention

And the angel of the Lord appeared unto him in a flame of fire out of the midst of a bush: and he looked, and, behold, the bush burned with fire, and the bush was not consumed. 3 And Moses said, I will now turn aside, and see this great sight, why the bush is not burnt. 4 And when the Lord saw that he turned aside to see, God called unto him out of the midst of the bush, and said, Moses, Moses. And he said, Here am I. Exodus 3:2-4

Week 19   **Day 4**

_____

_____

_____

_____

_____

_____

_____

_____

_____

_____

_____

_____

Prayer Focus: Use this time to stir the gifts in you because it part of God desires to use. Pray until your gifting is stirred again in you.

_____

_____

_____

_____

_____

_____

_____

_____

_____

_____

_____

_____

_____

_____

When God called Moses out of the bush Moses answered, "Here Am I." have you ever really thought about how vulnerable those word would make you? Now Moses does not see anybody, but does here a voice calling out to him yet he still says, **"Here am I"**. Will you answer though you are not sure it is God that is calling you? This is a call you have to answer by faith. When God calls out to you from the bush, He makes no promises, He gives no grand entrances nor does not say I am God. He merely calls your name twice and settles your call in heaven. Will you answer by faith?

94

When God Whispers Your To Capture Your Attention

And he said, Draw not nigh hither: put off thy shoes from off thy feet, for the place whereon thou standest is holy ground. 6 Moreover he said, I am the God of thy father, the God of Abraham, the God of Isaac, and the God of Jacob. And Moses hid his face; for he was afraid to look upon God. 7 And the Lord said, I have surely seen the affliction of my people which are in Egypt, and have heard their cry by reason of their taskmasters; for I know their sorrows; 8 And I am come down to deliver them out of the hand of the Egyptians, and to bring them up out of that land unto a good land and a large, unto a land flowing with milk and honey; Exodus 3:5-8

Week 19   Day 5 _____

Now that Moses has showed God that he is sensitive, understanding and willing to do what He desires, God tells Moses who He is. But God does not just say who He is, but rather gives Moses His covenant name. When God asks you to do something that involves you calling in the earth, He gives you His name to use in the earth as your identification badge. As you start the process of your assignment, will you do the assignment in your name or His name? Will it be your covenant with man, or your covenant with God? Make the decision that everything you do will be in His name and for His glory

Prayer Focus: God give me what I need for this next assignment and speak to me with clear details about it. I give my all to you and commit fully to your will.

95

Finishing Strong and Without Excuse

I have glorified thee on the earth: I have finished the work which thou gavest me to do. John 17:4

Week 20   **Day 1**

_____

_____

_____

_____

_____

_____

_____

_____

_____

_____

_____

_____

Prayer Focus: *Let your entire purpose this morning, in this intimate time be to question God. "God, have I completed my assignment? Is there anything that I have left undone?" Listen clearly and hear the truth from God as you wait in His presence.*

I know that by now you are feeling a sense of completion and are probably feel somewhat victorious. Even though it is a good thing to approach the finish line, don't let your guard down too soon. Be sure to complete everything that God has given you to complete. Your number one goal is to yield your best so that you may access His glory. Your life should be a flame of glory that God can appreciate. There may even be a fight of in your flesh where Satan is trying to defeat you one last time. It is important that you remember that what you tolerate you cannot dominate.

_____

_____

_____

_____

_____

_____

_____

_____

_____

_____

_____

_____

_____

_____

_____

_____

Finishing Strong and Without Excuse

And when we had finished our course from Tyre, we came to Ptolemais, and saluted the brethren, and abode with them one day. And as we tarried there many days, there came down from Judaea a certain prophet, named Agabus. And when he was come unto us, he took Paul's girdle, and bound his own hands and feet, and said, Thus saith the Holy Ghost, So shall the Jews at Jerusalem bind the man that owneth this girdle, and shall deliver him into the hands of the Gentiles. And when we heard these things, both we, and they of that place, besought him not to go up to Jerusalem. Acts 21:7, & 10-12

Week 20   **Day 2** _____

_____
I know that by now you are feeling _____
a sense of completion and you _____
probably feel somewhat victorious. _____
Have you ever gotten to the place _____
where you felt you had finally come _____
through a particular test or trying _____
period and found yourself right in _____
line for the next test? Don't ever _____
fear these periods of proving. God _____
is just declaring that you are indeed _____
worthy to be tried. Always remem- _____
ber that every exit out of something
is an entrance into something. It is
never an entrance into a lesser battle. It has to be greater so you can
increase at this next level without
hindrance. This is where you began
to exercise your spiritual mussel to
increase in a number of ways.

Prayer Focus: This completion is an entrance into something God deemed that you are prepared for. Therefore, declare a statement of faith just like the Apostle Paul did: "What mean ye to weep and to break mine heart? for I am ready not to be bound only, but also to die at Jerusalem for the name of the Lord Jesus." Ask God for the grace to endure the next test. Listen as God gives you this amazing word.

_____
_____
_____
_____
_____
_____
_____
_____
_____

97

Finishing Strong and Without Excuse

For we which have believed do enter into rest, as he said, As I have sworn in my wrath, if they shall enter into my rest: although the works were finished from the foundation of the world. Hebrews 4:3

Week 20   **Day 3**

_____
_____
_____
_____
_____
_____
_____
_____
_____
_____
_____
_____

Prayer Focus: *This is a day of declaration! Your goal must be to take what you want by faith through violence declaration. Remember what God said to Isaiah: "... Ask me of things to come concerning my sons, and concerning the work of my hands command ye me." Make a bold declaration regarding those things you desire!*

_____
_____
_____
_____
_____
_____
_____
_____
_____
_____
_____
_____
_____
_____
_____

Every time you win a battle you have come to the end of something and Satan tries you at a different level. Therefore, this type of an end always make you feel kind of good until you realize there is another test to take. The next test, however, will have to be won at the beginning and with a different mind that created the test. The only way to win at the beginning is to win by faith. Therefore, you cannot play into the trap of Satan and neither can you go for his bait. This simply means that you will have to enter a rest period, which will come through the joy of knowing that this battle was won from the foundation of the world. Winning sometimes means saying nothing because you know you have already won.

Finishing Strong and Without Excuse

And all the congregation worshipped, and the singers sang, and the trumpeters sounded: and all this continued until the burnt offering was finished.
2 Chronicles 29:28

Week 20   Day 4

Here we are feeling a sense of completion and we probably feel somewhat victorious. Yet we don't even realize there is still too much to our will for us to be anywhere near complete. We must keep in mind that God never considers you to be finished or complete until He sees you as an offering that is burned up for His glory. Until you are burned up, there will not be an end to your assignment no fulfilment of your test. You will remain at a place of worship, adding your voice to those who are singing and sounding the trumpet for the next battle. Let's go beyond where we are now and become an offering pour out for the glory of God. Empty yourself until there is nothing left of you. We all need to see the you that no one has ever met, not even you.

Prayer Focus: There is so much to live for and, because of that, we need to know what is left to die to. After the battle, you need a fresh touch of His presence. That touching will only come through worship. Therefore, enter into a place of worship and watch what God will say to you before this day is over.

99

Finishing Strong and Without Excuse

I have fought a good fight, I have finished my course, I have kept the faith:
2 Timothy 4:7

_____ **Week 20**   **Day 5**

_____

_____

_____

_____

_____

_____

_____

_____

_____

_____

Prayer Focus: The Bible tells us "if you draw nigh to God, He will draw nigh to you". Let's focus on finding out how we can draw closer to God so that we might find Him drawing closer to us and so that we might experience the fullness of the splendor/glory of God.

_____

_____

_____

_____

_____

_____

_____

_____

_____

_____

_____

_____

_____

_____

As we are coming down this last lap of a successful prayer and worship experience, let's boast about what God has done. God is a God of faith, purpose Design and objectivity. If Paul is able to say he has kept the faith, what that says to me is that he would never let go of God will he ever let go of what God desire of him. If we will ever be in a position to boast about what God has done, we must be able to say "I have finished my course, I have kept the faith now there is laid of up for me a crown of righteousness." It is at this point that God will be glorified. Many of give up and quit much too soon and God never get the glory from our lives. We simply never Give Our Best For His Glory. If you dare to give your best I promise you God will share his glory with you. The glory God will share is the splendor and manifestation of all God is.

Celebrating With a Crown Won

I have fought a good fight, I have finished my course, I have kept the faith: 8Henceforth there is laid up for me a crown of righteousness, which the Lord, the righteous judge, shall give me at that day: and not to me only, but unto all them also that love his appearing. 2 Timothy 4:7-8

Week 21   Day 1 _____

Every time you get to the place that you finish something, God get to the place that he starts to fill up his bag of rewards. God will pour out blessings on us if we would dare to finish what we start. The blessing of God normally has something to do with authority backed by anointing. God's waiting right now for you to cross the finish line so that He would be able to favor you and grant you an anointing that is proof of your victory. The greatest level of favor and anointing comes to those that finish. Because you have dared to not only finish the course at this level of challenge but also create a place for God to dwell. God will do for you what you have not imagined. You have also finished this 21 week prayer consecration that has so increased you in your prayer experience and intimate moments with God and that calls for favor on your life.

Prayer Focus: When favor comes, that's a good time to thank God for what you believe that you receive that you have already asked for in times past that has not yet manifested. Because you have finished, go and get what you have been after in God and in this natural world. This is the time of favor for those that have finished. Ask God what does He want you to go after and don't think small.

101

Celebrating With a Crown Won

And said, My Lord, if now I have found favour in thy sight, pass not away, I pray thee, from thy servant: Genesis 18:3

Week 21 **Day 2**

_____
_____
_____
_____
_____
_____
_____
_____
_____
_____
_____
_____

Prayer Focus: *God, will you go with me? If I have found favor in your sight, go with me as you went with Moses? Use your covenant that you have which is better than the old covenant.*

_____
_____
_____
_____
_____
_____
_____
_____
_____
_____
_____
_____
_____
_____

One of the rewards that you will have is that the Lord will not leave you. In any given situation you request the Lord's presence, He abides with you because you have found favor in His sight. Where would you like God to go with you in light of His presence? Favor will cause Him to go with you. If we would have God to go with us, then to what degree are you willing to go with and for God? Think about Elisha, he went with Elijah sometimes even against all odds. There were those that seem to be gifted Prophets that tried to deter him from continuing to follow. I am sure you have them as well. When you attempt to finish anything, Satan always sends those that have the purpose to discourage you from following who you are called to. But if you continue, you will be able to decree what you desire.

102

Celebrating With a Crown Won

And if thou deal thus with me, kill me, I pray thee, out of hand, if I have found favour in thy sight; and let me not see my wretchedness.16And the LORD said unto Moses, Gather unto me seventy men of the elders of Israel, whom thou knowest to be the elders of the people, and officers over them; and bring them unto the tabernacle of the congregation, that they may stand there with thee.
Numbers 11:15-16

Week 21   Day 3

Every time you get to the place that you finish something, God get to the place that He may fill up His bag of rewards. When you come to the place of the reward, God will cause favor to follow you to the point where you can ask Him for people and He will give them the heart to follow you. That is called the favor of God. The word says He will give men for thee. And men that God will give, your favor will come on them. When God gives you people, of course, that means another level of responsibility for you.

Here you are with the responsibility of more people because you have been faithful. What will you give them and where will you take them that they have not already been? Anytime God gives you people, He always directs you where you must bring them. Bringing them or taking them requires something you to have more than you have had in the past.

Prayer Focus: God please make my eyes to look right on that I will be able to select the right people to help me with what you called me to do, and I will be able to take them where you instruct me. I need your favor, wisdom and understanding to do so. Through favor I will make the right decisions. Pray now for what you lacking that is necessary for you to help people.

Celebrating With a Crown Won

Now when the turn of Esther, the daughter of Abihail the uncle of Mordecai, who had taken her for his daughter, was come to go in unto the king, she required nothing but what Hegai the king's chamberlain, the keeper of the women, appointed. And Esther obtained favour in the sight of all them that looked upon her. Esther 2:15

Week 21   **Day 4**

_____

_____

_____

_____

_____

_____

_____

_____

_____

_____

_____

Prayer Focus: *God, who can I bless today as a symbol of my faith in the favor that you have bestowed on me? God what would like for me to do for you today?*

Every time you get to the place that you finish something God get to the place that He may open up His bag of rewards. Esther had favor with all that she came in contact with. When we finish, God grants such a level of favor that everyone would recognize what's on you. The blessing is in finishing. At your finishing line, God holds your stuff for you. That stuff is called favor, anointing, gifting and honor. But isn't it sometimes so hard to finish? As you are coming down the home stretch of the test, challenge, race or whatever it is, haven't you noticed that it is at that time things gets harder? Why is that? It is because Satan doesn't desire to see you with the prize because that would mean he failed. His job was to stop you and he could not do it. When you finish, it is proof that you have unstoppable faith!

Celebrating With a Crown Won

Thou shalt arise, and have mercy upon Zion: for the time to favour her, yea, the set time, is come.   Psalm 102:13

Week 21   Day 5

There are times that you think that you did not finish with all honor, but you did finish. God is more concerned in your finishing than He is in your mistakes. What God has in His thinking is since you have finished, the time to favor you has come, yea the set time. This kind of favor causes the blessings of God to run you down. Many times we don't consider what we are missing by not finishing. Every time we neglect to finish something, we miss seeing our obedience manifested. Esther finished and got a crown, Ruth finished and got a Boaz, Abraham finished and got a Son in his old age and Jesus finished and got a throne. What will you miss if you don't finish? Everyone you see in the Bible that finished received something and those that quit received nothing.

Prayer Focus: Be sensitive as God prepares to bless you. The blessing may show up in a way that you think not. You may be looking for money and it shows up in the anointing. I speak God's richest blessing on your life that you possibly handle. I pray the richest prophetic anointing on you that you can possibly handle. May the Lord be with you always to enrich you in knowledge, wisdom, and understanding of the Word and that He may increase you forever.

105

"Jeremiah 1:9-10 (KJV) 9 Then the LORD put forth his hand, and touched my mouth. And the LORD said unto me, Behold, I have put my words in thy mouth. 10 See, I have this day set thee over the nations and over the kingdoms, to root out, and to pull down, and to destroy, and to throw down, to build, and to plant.

Bishop Rodney S. Walker I is a dynamic prophetic voice whose ministry is renowned as being a catalytic agent for understanding and maturing in the prophetic.

A native of Washington, D.C., Bishop Walker is the Founder and Senior Pastor of Heritage Church International, established in 1990 in Waldorf, Maryland. He serves as the General Overseer of Bishop R. S. Walker Ministries - formerly Another Touch of Glory Ministries - that covers national and international churches, para-church ministries and businesses.

He is spiritually covered by and accountable to Dr. Michael Freeman of Spirit of Faith Christian Center in Temple Hills, Maryland. He is also submitted to his Spiritual Father, Bishop Ralph L. Dennis of Kingdom Fellowship Covenant Ministries in Towson, Maryland.

In addition to being a graduate of the Jericho Christian Training College, Bishop R.S.Walker received his Doctor of Divinity degree from The Spirit of Truth Institute. Bishop R. S. Walker's training by versatile and equipped instructors, guidance from his Mentor, as well as submission to his Spiritual Father, has developed him into a well-balanced, grounded, and seasoned prophet.

On July 19, 1997, Bishop Walker was ordained Elder in the Office of Prophet by Kingdom Fellowship Covenant Ministries. In 1999, Bishop Walker founded the School of the Prophets. The School has locations in Waldorf and Baltimore, MD, Raleigh and Wilson, NC, Abuja, Nigeria, York, Pa, and has been hosted throughout the United States and beyond using online streaming.

March 15, 2002, Bishop Walker completed the coursework for the Joint College of African-American Pentecostal Bishops Congress and July 3, 2009 was Ordained and Consecrated in the Office of Bishop by Kingdom Fellowship Covenant Ministries.

In addition to equipping and training in the prophetic, Bishop Walker has also assembled a body of Prophetic Presbyters who assist him in managing the great assignment God has set to his hands.

Bishop Walker is the author and publisher of over 10 books including: *The Prophetic Prayer Journal, Raising Prophets of Character, Becoming a Proven Prophetic Voice, The 21st Century Prophet, The Renaissance Prophet, and The Father/Son Encounter* all of which prove to be phenomenal resources of the serious believer's library.

Among Bishop Walker's many accomplishments, is that of being a devoted husband to his lovely wife, Pastor Betty Walker, and a loving father to his eleven wonderful children.

Bishop Rodney S. Walker's ultimate goal is to fulfill all that God has purposed for his life and to effectively lead those placed in his prophetic and pastoral care. His love for God is evident in his preaching, teaching and zeal for ministry. You will experience the wind of the Spirit through this Man of God.

Visit www.bishoprswalkerproducts.com for additional Bishop RS Walker products including prophetic CD's, DVD's Books, ebooks and more.

Creating a Paradigm of Spiritual Fathering While Leaving a Legacy of Apostolic and Prophetic Leadership

2760 Crain Highway Waldorf, MD 20601
office (301) 843-9267 fax (240) 585-7093
www.bishoprswalkerproducts.com
admin@bishoprswalker.com

www.ingramcontent.com/pod-product-compliance
Lightning Source LLC
Chambersburg PA
CBHW060024050426
42448CB00012B/2865